Jea Cocteau
x 1954

SCANDAL & PARADE:

The Theater of

JEAN COCTEAU

NEAL OXENHANDLER

RUTGERS UNIVERSITY PRESS

NEW BRUNSWICK, NEW JERSEY, 1957

Second Printing, 1969

The author acknowledges the following permissions to
quote from the works of Jean Cocteau: Editions du Rocher
for *La Difficulté d'être;* Librairie Stock for *Orphée* and
Le Rappel à l'ordre; Editions Bernard Grasset and Jean
Cocteau for *Portraits-Souvenirs, La Machine infernale,
Journal d'un inconnu* and *Lettre aux Américains;* and
Librairie Gallimard for *Bacchus, Les Parents terribles,
Les Mariés de la Tour Eiffel, Antigone, Les Chevaliers
de la Table Ronde, Renaud et Armide, La Machine à écrire,
L'Aigle à deux têtes, Les Monstres sacrés* and *Maalesh.*
All translations were made by the author.

TO MY MOTHER AND FATHER

ACKNOWLEDGMENTS

THE EXISTENCE OF THIS BOOK IS DUE IN LARGE PART TO HENRI Peyre of Yale, whose belief in the stature of Cocteau was a strong and forthright encouragement. I am also grateful to those colleagues and friends at Yale who helped me at all stages with the doctoral dissertation from which parts of the present book are taken. Jean Boorsch and Jacques Guicharnaud helped with their knowledge both of Cocteau and of the theater. Kenneth Douglas, by judicious and patient criticism, helped me take the long step from conception to communication. I am indebted also to Marcel Mendelson, Thomas M. Greene and Robert J. Nelson, who read the manuscript at varying stages. My wife frequently demonstrated the infallibility of feminine intuition in her readings of the manuscript. Finally, I should like to express an old debt of gratitude to Wallace Fowlie, who first spoke to me of Cocteau, made him a living presence and a riddle worth solving.

Situation of Cocteau

"The theater's nobility is compounded of mystery."

Le Foyer des Artistes

JEAN COCTEAU, WHO IS NOW AN OLD MAN, HAS ONE OF THE supreme qualities of youth. He remains virtually indefinable. Eric Bentley suggests that this is due to the "awful vacuity" of his work.[1] Cocteau has been seen by other critics as an inspired clown, a carnival magician, a dilettante and a faker; in short, anything but a serious writer. Others, young men too close to the poet and too susceptible to his personal charm, have risen to his defense with arguments culled from his own pages. They have usually succeeded in making their idol more vulnerable, and, in any case, they have not clarified the difficulties which the works of Jean Cocteau present.

One of the first problems in the appreciation of Cocteau is a problem of language. This was clearly seen by Jacques Rivière: "M. Cocteau is a poet . . . his book is no more than a parade, in the memory, of the subtlest metaphors . . . wherein his ideas are so well costumed that we no longer recognize them." [2] Rivière, like Bentley, seems to suggest that Cocteau's metaphors are empty and vacuous, that they disguise a lack of meaning, rather than a fullness which must be expressed in the rich and ambiguous complexities of figurative language. At any rate, some rational counterpart, which would amplify and explain the metaphors, seems to be lacking. This accounts for the fact that those critics who have attempted to explain Cocteau by merely repeating his own metaphors and the explanations which he gives of them have not cast much light on the works. The explanations themselves are nothing but a metaphorical shorthand.

The difficulties of Cocteau's works are not, however, merely stylistic; while differing with Bentley and Rivière on the vacuity of Cocteau's production, we must nevertheless admit that this is a hermetic universe which does not easily yield up its secrets. Cocteau is very conscious of this hermetic aspect; he points to it by a central metaphor which recurs throughout his work, the evocation of "mystery." Again and again, in his poetry, his plays, his criticism, Cocteau returns to this obsessive theme.

In *Orphée* (1926), he is concerned with the mystery of death: "*Orphée* is the first time that anyone has ever shown night [that is, death] in full daylight."[3] In his *Lettre à Jacques Maritain* (1928), the term mystery takes on a more Christian character. "Since 1913 I had been living and dying of mystery in disorder. *Le Potomak* proves it. During that period I trained myself to dream. . . . Before discovering this simple thing: God, the order of mystery—what disorder! How many traps did I set for it! Mystery was my *idée fixe*."[4]

Mystery, which he now calls "invisibility," is the main theme of one of Cocteau's most recent works, *Journal d'un inconnu* (1953). In this most abstract and analytical of all his books, he tries to establish a philosophy of mystery. There is the mystery of poetry, associated with the idea of purity; and the mystery of the poet himself, which is his "invisibility." The whole universe is mysterious, and Cocteau retreats, finally, to a kind of resigned skepticism. Perhaps the mystery cannot be explained at all; his mystery, as an individual, is inherent in the greater mystery of the universe. "The mistake must have been to try to understand what goes on in every story of the building."[5]

These quotations suggest that mystery for Cocteau is a protean term of many and changing meanings. Although we shall be concerned, throughout this study, with further specifications of Cocteau's mystery, it is possible at this point to suggest a global significance for the term which underlies all the particular mysteries of the works. The fundamental reason for the mystery of Cocteau's works—a mystery which he has chosen and which is perhaps his hallmark as an artist—is an absence of "situation" which is found on all levels throughout his entire production.

The forces which drive Cocteau's characters relate to no context, either in the work or in the world, which might generalize these characters and relate them to society and history. This is a dramatic and poetic world whose most vital concerns remain below the surface, are deflected and suppressed, so that they express themselves only in highly metaphorical and allegorical forms which dimly shadow forth their true meaning. Although Cocteau's universe might be compared to that of Proust as a microcosm of the neurotic spirit struggling to escape from its shackles and contradictions, there is no framework or perspective, such as that which Proust provides in his novel, which justifies this universe and shows its relation to human history. There is no transcendence or universalization in Cocteau comparable to Proust's theory of remembrance or the enormous framework of generalities which is built on the plots of his novel. With the exception perhaps of the naturalistic *Parents terribles,* Cocteau's opus is suspended in time and space. He does not relate his plays to our world, the everyday world of which all art must, in some fashion, be a criticism.

The suspended condition of Cocteau's art, the ambiguity of his style and the ambivalence of his characters determine his philosophical position, his view of man, art and world. This is, generally speaking, a form of poetic idealism. No reduction of Cocteau's dramatic universe to a philosophical system is intended, however; indeed, such a reduction would be impossible for the reason that the main motive power or concern in all of Cocteau's works is a psychological one.

The problem which Cocteau's plays would solve is not philosophical; their drama is never raised to the level of ideas. The moral and ethical are not at issue here. There is no social or political concern. Nor is any distinction made between an action motivated by moral choice and a purely obsessive one. Even the broader issue of man's nature and place in the universe is mere backdrop. It is the changing scenery before which the drama of the Self is acted. The way in which the Self is envisaged suggests his important connections with poetic idealism. But idealism is not at stake; it is not going to be demonstrated or proved; it is only part of the atmosphere of Cocteau's plays. Cocteau shows no fidelity to idealism. Indeed, he finds its trammels heavy and, ultimately, limiting to the man and the playwright he would be.

The psychological motive which animates Cocteau's plays is the source of their unity. Without writing biography or falling into the trap of "psychologistic" criticism, we might say that the name "Cocteau" is the sign of the work's unity. It is not the author, the man, whom we are trying to explain by means of such a procedure, but the principle which operates on the literary materials.

There is also a second sense in which we are interested in the presence of the author in his work: that is, as the "dramatic speaker," the narrator or commentator, or, more simply, the source of the play's point of view. Cocteau himself ironically anticipates this kind of inquiry by actually inserting his name into one of the plays: the statue in *Orphée* tells the police commissioner that its name is Jean Cocteau and gives the author's address. Point of view is closely related to the kind of self-consciousness and, ultimately, the very conception of theater found in the plays of Cocteau.

The approach which I shall sometimes employ here bears a resemblance to the "Existential psychoanalysis" of Jean-Paul Sartre. The problem of liberty is a central one for Sartre; and, as we shall see, liberty is also a vital concern in Cocteau. The themes of persecution and of alienation, from society and from Self, are central to the Sartrian analyses of Baudelaire and Jean Genet, as they are to the line of thought which I propose to follow in examining Cocteau. Perhaps even more valuable than Sartre's critical method is his ethical position. His conception of involvement or "engagement" provides a useful moral and historical vantage point from which to study Cocteau.

This is not, I repeat, psychologism. And it therefore seems necessary to differ from Sartre on one important point. Sartre makes no distinction between the biography and the literary work. In this book I shall attempt to concern myself with the author *as he appears in his works*. For, as Cocteau himself says in *Portraits-Souvenirs,* we cannot descend very far into the darkness of an individual soul. Following his example in that book, I disclaim any intention to violate the "tombs of Egypt" or unwrap any "sacred bandages."

Finally, lest it be thought that this study would deny Cocteau's stature as a playwright, I have attempted to show that there is, in fact, a form of commitment in these plays, a commitment to negation which provides its own powerful dramatic impact; it arises not merely from personal psychological causes but from the very cultural and historical context in which Cocteau functioned as man and artist.

I hope that the pages which follow will enlighten the mystery of Cocteau without destroying it and that some of the paradoxes of his life and art will arrange themselves into that meaningful patterning of mysteries which we call by the hopeful name of knowledge.

The entre
deux guerres

JEAN COCTEAU IS ONE OF THE LAST REPRESENTATIVES OF A GREAT literary generation. Along with Picasso, Mauriac and a few others, Cocteau symbolizes a period of intense artistic activity and discovery, one of the most fertile in the entire history of French literature, which spans the years between the two world wars. And perhaps more than any other single man, Cocteau is the spokesman for this period. He has repeatedly tried to explain it, to remake it, to justify it, to catch it forever in the stasis of an epigram. Each one of his works shapes the destiny of this period and writes its history. Cocteau's own virtues and his limitations are those of the *entre deux guerres*. Even his most strenuous intellectual efforts at rejuvenation have not changed him fundamentally. He has deepened but he has not changed. Frivolity, poetry, style, moral courage and cowardice, the highest tragedy and the most abject self-deception, are to be found in Cocteau's writings, his paintings and the memoirs of his personal relationships with his contemporaries. All the facets of his work focus in a single image, but it is not Cocteau who is seen in this multiple mirror but the entire history of his age, complex, baffling, foolish and wise. Unlike the historian or the critic who merely catalogues the variety of historical phenomena, Cocteau has tried to reconcile the forms of the age within himself and express them in a poem or a play. Nor is Cocteau a *pasticheur;* his works have their own authenticity and express a truth which is peculiarly their own.

Cocteau has always needed strong personalities around him; yet, at the same time, he has managed to defend himself against them. We find in his work only curious and fragmentary vestiges of his many spiritual and artistic attachments. He has absorbed all the rest, put his stamp on it and made it his own. Like Galaad in his play *Les Chevaliers de la Table Ronde,* Cocteau has searched for the grail of self-knowledge, doing battle with monsters and false prophets, wrestling with angels, interrogating demons. Many of his closest friends are "monstres sacrés," public figures with doctrines and programs, with public personalities. Cocteau speaks of them with love and hate, jealousy and generosity; he exorcises one and allows himself to be possessed by another. The pendulum swings across his life and his work, the tragedian puts on a comic mask; but, in the last act, it is Cocteau who appears on the stage, carrying the carcass of the Sphinx on his shoulder and repeating the magic formula which he has learned in the dark descent into his own soul. Cocteau, like any true artist, is both within and beyond literary history. If in this chapter the emphasis is on his attempts to synthesize Mallarmé and Gide, music and poetry, pantomime and the dance, it is only to prepare us for an examination of that synthesis in its own right, as an object of art, with its own autonomous existence and truth.

The period of the *entre deux guerres* embodies a gamut of values, from frivolity to tragic sobriety, and Cocteau's career reflects the same scale. Like Proust, Cocteau began as a frivolous esthete, a pampered social butterfly. At the precocious age of sixteen, Cocteau became the darling of the literary salons. The famous actor Edouard de Max gave a public reading of the boy's poetry; he moved in aristocratic society, mingled with princes, diplomats, actors and actresses. For a time, the young Cocteau was only too ready to accept this easy success as a valid judgment of his work. But soon he began to be ashamed of himself and his meaningless triumphs among the snobs and esthetes who were seduced by his poetic appearance rather than his first books of verse, *La Lampe d'Aladin* and *Le Prince frivole*.

He was in his twenties when he began to develop along more

serious lines, gaining inspiration from the severe artistry of Serge Diaghilev and Nijinsky of the Ballet Russe, the composer Erik Satie, the poet Guillaume Apollinaire, Picasso and the other Montmartre painters who were in the midst of their revolution. These artists, daring and original, yet masters of technique, exacting in their demands on themselves and their public, provided Cocteau with an inspiring image of the artistic life, its importance and the sacrifices it entailed.

It was at this time that Cocteau began to consider himself a poet and that he undertook, at first in a very superficial way, to assume the responsibilities and privileges of the poet's vocation. Cocteau has known intimately almost all the great creative personalities of his generation, men who triumphantly reaffirmed the supremacy of artistic creation. The whole meaning of Cocteau's personality and his interpretation of the world are tied up with creativity, with poetry. In an age wracked by doubts, this was the one thing that Cocteau never doubted. His belief in the value of poetry and the authenticity of his vocation are constantly reaffirmed through, and often in spite of, the shifting allegiances which seem to be the rule of his nature.

The period of which we are speaking—that period between the two wars which Cocteau so perfectly represents—might well be called the age of expressionism. It was an age which made the artistic vocation supreme and analogized from the nature of artistic experience to all other aspects of life. Its morals were the morals of Gide, with his emphasis on the truth of perception and the ambiguity of action. Jacques Maritain and Henri Brémond linked poetry with religious experience. Bergson discussed the vital role of intuition in cultural evolution. Surrealism, Futurism and German Expressionism affirmed the values of subjectivity as against the dubious realities of a world whose very existence had long since been put in doubt by Kant and Hegel. This was the period of Croce, the philosopher of expressionism. Wagner, who conceived of music primarily as the expression of the inner being, was still in vogue. Throughout all Europe the supremacy of the inner being, the Self, was the theme of all the arts and of philosophy. This was the epoch of post-Hegelianism which reversed the ancient realism of the Renaissance and taught that the Self created its own world. The age of expressionism was the apogee of Romanticism, out of which it developed. It flourished and died during the period between the two wars. The sense of new things to come is already implicit in the award of the prix Goncourt, in 1933, to André Malraux's *La Condition humaine.*

In literature alone, the forms of this expressionism are extremely varied. But the basic emphasis is always on the Self, a Self which exists most completely in the form of artistic expression and which, through this expression, creates about itself a world which has a greater validity than the everyday world of common sense. The early works of Maurice Barrès and all the works of André Gide provide us with a fundamentally expressionistic image of life. These two men played an important part in Cocteau's intellectual development, as they did in that of most young men of his generation.

It was in 1889, the year of Cocteau's birth, that Maurice Barrès published *Un Homme libre.* a testimony to the supremacy of sensation in the development of the inner Self, the *Moi*. Despite the conversion of Barrès, relatively early, to an entrenched conservatism, the book remains as the first testimony to a new spiritual movement. Cocteau has said: "But what Barrès affirmed as a young man has not yet been contradicted." [1] After Barrès it was André Gide who began to expound the new doctrine of moral and intellectual freedom; and, indeed, that freedom was the call to arms of the writers of all Europe who saw their world shattered by a war which they felt had been imposed on them and which solved nothing. Freedom took many forms. In the Barrès of *Le Culte du Moi* and in all of Gide's work, it appeared chiefly as a new spontaneity of the sensibility and the emotions, a freedom, above all, from the traditional moral sense which has always reigned supreme in French life and thought.

There is little apparent similarity between the works of Cocteau and Barrès. But although their works differ in form, there is a vein of irony common to both. Both of them, as Cocteau puts it, "make fun of something while respecting it." [2] There is a fundamental distrust of even their most public allegiances and enthusiasms to which this irony is often the only clue.

Nor does the outward form of Cocteau's works much resemble that of Gide's. Gide's best writing, even such an apparently objective novel as *Les Faux Monnayeurs,* is confessional. He is constantly crying out to his readers to understand him, to participate with him in the joys of the flesh or the imagination. And the cry has a kind of pathos about it which pierces through the man's defensive irony, because he suspects that his readers will ultimately reject his message. Cocteau, on the other hand, has written very little about himself. He has preferred to remain anonymous behind the plots of his novels or his plays. Yet his fundamental problem, as we shall see it emerge through an examination of his plays, is close to Gide's, although more elliptically expressed.

Striking a kind of Gidian pose, Cocteau has said: "The intense sincerity of each minute, even when it offers a series of apparent contradictions, traces a straighter, a deeper line than all the theoretical lines to which one is often forced to sacrifice the best part of oneself." [3] This sentence is taken from Cocteau's portrait of Maurice Barrès. It suggests the belief, common to both Barrès and Gide, that the intensity of experience is our only truth, and that this reality of the emotions, which is the only reality that we can claim, must not be sacrificed to any arbitrarily imposed system of morality.

Although he was capable of expressing the idea, Cocteau did not come to the conclusion that freedom was an end in itself until much later. His freedom was as uneasy as that of Barrès, and, one by one, he tried out the alternatives to freedom. But even more than most of the men of his generation who for a time took Gide as their spokesman, Cocteau was to discover that freedom was the very essence of his nature. Ultimately, freedom became destructive for Cocteau, as it did for Gide, and for a similar reason. Because the world would not accept them, or so they felt, they would not accept the world, and the resultant denial of commitment involved them in emotional and artistic subterfuges which were damaging to them. This is not to deny them the nobility of an attitude lived uncompromisingly. Cocteau's life and work constitute a restless search, impelled by a fervor to discover and a skeptical inability to accept which are unique in all of French literature.

It is indeed typical of Cocteau that after Barrès and Gide the next of his great intellectual guides was Jacques Maritain. The opium habit had taken a strong grip on Cocteau after the death of Raymond Radiguet in 1923. While Cocteau was undergoing a cure, he and a number of his friends came under the influence of Maritain. Cocteau saw in Maritain the very opposite of Gide: a life based on commitment. Here was a man whose wisdom and personal integrity arose out of the acceptance of a limiting situation. Again, it was the call of a strong personality, and Cocteau succumbed. On May 21, 1926, Cocteau received the sacrament from the saintly Père Charles at Maritain's home in Meudon. So, for a brief time, he was a member of that group of converts to Catholicism which centered around Maritain and included, or was to include, such men as Henri Ghéon, Francis Jammes, Pierre Reverdy and Jacques Copeau.

All of these men found in Maritain a spiritual leader and—equally important—an esthetician. Although their philosophical orientation was in the direction of Thomistic realism, it was a realism which accorded a large place to the mystery of art with its double nature, its concreteness and its spirituality. For these men the issue of the moral influence of art, which has frequently caused repression of the arts during periods of religious fervor, was a minor consideration compared with the resources of art as a privileged form of cognition. There is even a kind of expressionism implicit in the esthetics of Maritain.

The poetic faculty, for Maritain, is not the mere craftsmanship of the artisan which might be suggested by his emphasis on the poem as artifact. Poetry is intelligence using feeling, shaping the world of things, by an act in which both Self and thing are transformed into the poetic sign. Such terms as "creative intuition" and "spiritual intelligence" point to the role of subjectivity in his esthetics. While Maritain never abandons his Thomistic realism, his esthetics point to the element of mystery in poetry, that element—spiritual, intuitive, unconscious or divine—which is emphasized by all the more conventional theorists of expressionism.

In 1928 Cocteau broke publicly with the Maritain group over the issue of Jean Desborde's *J'Adore,* for which Cocteau had written the preface and for which he carried on an unremitting campaign of publicity. The book was replete with adolescent masturbation fantasies which scandalized even Maritain's enlightened circle. It was probably fitting that the emotional life was the issue over which Cocteau broke with Maritain and his Catholic friends. Cocteau must have felt that his emotional salvation could not be found within the dogmas of Christianity. He had been attracted by Maritain himself and the nostalgic appeal of the Catholicism of his youth, but his whole inner orientation, which he had not yet explored and did not yet understand, was carrying him in other and lonelier directions.

Robert Merle has made a brilliant analysis of the conversions of Oscar Wilde, Cocteau, Verlaine and Maurice Sachs in a recent number of *Les Temps modernes.* He explains these conversions as an attempt on the part of men who feel themselves outlawed from society (in this case by homosexuality) to belong to the human community and, at the same time, recognize, in terms of an objective system exterior to themselves, their strong inner sense of guilt.

Cocteau was never, literally speaking, a member of any school, unless it be the ephemeral *esprit nouveau* movement launched by his friend Guillaume Apollinaire with the manifesto *L'Esprit nouveau et les poètes,* published after the first world war. The theory of the *esprit nouveau* was expressed with a laudable vagueness by Apollinaire, who had about him nothing of the dogmatism of André Breton, the high priest of Surrealism. Apollinaire was feeling his own way, trying to express his own sense of poetry and certain tendencies which he felt represented the esthetic currents of his period. The *esprit nouveau* was really a frame of mind, a new sense of freedom in the choice of subject matter and poetic devices. It directed the poet to the inherent poetry in the life about him and tried to free him from the inherited conventions and viewpoints of tradition. Like Baudelaire, Apollinaire was looking for poetry in the clutter and agitation of daily life. But unlike Baudelaire, he wanted to find the forms which would be suitable for such a theme. He was not satisfied with the conventions of the past. There was optimism in Apollinaire, a belief in man and in poetry, which is, above all, the source of his lyrical power. Even through his melancholy poems on love or on war there emerges a sense of rightness, that even this suffering is as it should be—a deep and human joy.

Cocteau, too, was optimistic about poetry, about what it could do for men if they would only let it. But they, alas, would not. And so Cocteau, harking back to the more somber Romantics and Baudelaire, is deeply pessimistic about human nature. However, his most lighthearted play, *Les Mariés de la Tour Eiffel,* closely resembles Apollinaire's *Les Mamelles de Tirésias.* The same farcical spirit prevails; the same kind of unexpected and improvised poetry kindles the action. Cocteau took from Apollinaire a sense of freedom in the manipulation of syntax and choice of vocabulary. His use of language, like Apollinaire's, is highly inventive.

Cocteau declared in *Opium,* in 1930: "The true masters of the youth of 1912–1930 were Rimbaud, Ducasse, Nerval, Sade." [4] These *poètes maudits* were brought to fashion neither by Gide nor by Apollinaire. They were the household gods of a new movement, emerging contemporaneously with the *esprit nouveau,* a movement with a philosophy and a cult—Surrealism. Although the Surrealists were, for many years, bitter enemies of all that Cocteau represented, he seems to have taken as much from them as from his personal friend, Apollinaire.

Three main forces lie behind Surrealism. Perhaps the most important was German Romanticism, in which the exploration of the Self had already begun. World War I added a pretext, a new impetus to turn inward, away from the chaos of organized society. And the popularization of the works of Sigmund

Freud gave the Surrealist writers a method. They explored the subconscious only to find that man was inherently a creature of violence and contradiction. The turmoil was not merely the result of history, of the war, which most men considered the cause of their suffering and of the disintegration of society. The turmoil was essential to the human condition; it was permanent and metaphysical.

Gide, like the Surrealists, was an apostle of contradiction. But there remains in Gide, for all his modernism, a strong sense of classical values, a conviction that through our very contradiction, truth and beauty will emerge. The Surrealists, like the German Expressionists, are already of another generation. For them, contradiction is a value in and for itself. The very stuff of human nature seems to manifest a primitive and uncontrollable violence. Cocteau, in this sense, is quite far from the Surrealists, although he resembles them in his belief in scandal and the use of poetry as a revolutionary anti-bourgeois weapon. Cocteau, too, has urged his readers to awaken to the mysterious depths of their own beings and to accept responsibility for whatever angel or demon they may find there. For the most part, however, his "scandals" have been literary and esthetic—the ballet *Parade* and the disturbing *Parents terribles*. Nor was Cocteau as free as the Surrealists. His work is pondered, rewritten, constricted by intellectual indecision and a persistent groping for artistic form. Moreover, Cocteau was far from being sufficiently subversive to please the Surrealists. In a typical blast of character assassination André Breton pontificated: "Paul Claudel and . . . Cocteau, authors of infamous patriotic poems, of nauseous Catholic professions of faith, ignominious profiteers of the regime and confirmed counterrevolutionaries." [5] For many years the Surrealists were Cocteau's bitter personal foes, and he never participated—indeed, would not have been allowed to participate—in their manifestos or *cénacles*.

Cocteau did not have much respect for the Italian Futurists: "Marinetti charms us like a peddler, by the multicolored balls that he throws against the ruins, the trembling that he imprints on the ancient Italian *far niente*." [6] This perhaps does the Futurists justice. There was an element of dilettantism in all their productions, and they never had the violent intensity of purpose of the Surrealists or their German counterparts, the Expressionists.

There is a blood kinship between Dada, Futurism, Surrealism and German Expressionism, for the passions generated by the war seem to have marked all Europeans in much the same way. These movements were violent rejections of postwar society, and their hope for a new order was based on the awakening of secret, uncivilized forces in man. All had in common an intense subjectiveness, an orientation inward, rather than outward. Speaking of the Expressionist writer, Lotte Eisner says: "Man has ceased to be an individual tied to a duty, a morality, a family, a society. The Expressionist's life surpasses all superficial logic and the principle of causality. Released from all bourgeois remorse, admitting only the prodigious barometer of his sensibility, he abandons himself to his impulses. . . . We create reality, the image of the world exists only in us." [7] Nor was this a sudden break with tradition. It was a renewal of the poetic idealism of Mallarmé and Rilke, although more destructive. The implicit denial of reality in Mallarmé and Rilke became a precept of action for the Surrealists and Expressionists, whose works and lives are full of undisguised violence and hostility to the world around them.

There are relevant comparisons to be made here between Cocteau and the Expressionists, for the latter are best known for their works on stage and screen. They tackled, as did Cocteau, the task of transforming the new ideas and emotions into characters and plots, and they tried to express them in a comprehensible language, suitable for the stage. Cocteau was familiar with Expressionistic movies, and he must have seen at least several Expressionistic plays produced in translation in the avant-garde theaters of Paris.

In his own plays, Cocteau has in common with the Expressionists a foreshortening of character. The characters do not have the fullness or roundness that we have learned to expect in the heroes of the classic or the naturalistic drama. They are vehicles of ideas or personifications of a single obsession which they repeatedly act out with a dreamlike monotony. In all but *Les Parents terribles,* his most important naturalistic play, the characters are fictions rather than psychological entities. Like the fleeing bank clerk of Georg Kaiser's *From Morn till Midnight,* Cocteau's heroes plunge through a series of unreal landscapes dialoguing with themselves until the curtain closes on them like the lid of a box on a marionette. They are in a zone of amorous ambiguity, of sexual malaise, like the heroes and heroines of Franz Wedekind. Most important of all is the resolute subjectivism of these plays. Like the heroes of Expressionism, Cocteau's heroes are all in rebellion, struggling to affirm the power of struggle, an autistic apotheosis wherein the Self may be and know itself to be even as it is destroyed by the world.

Cocteau's careful prose resembles the concise so-called telegram or letter style of the Expressionists. The cubistic stage settings of Ernst Toller's social protest plays anticipate the abstract quality of certain Cocteau sets. Cocteau's drawings and the masks and decorations which he has devised for some of his plays are convulsive, like the paintings of Oskar Kokoschka, or quietly mysterious, like the works of Max Beckmann. The dream quality of Fritz Von Unruh's plays is similar to the unreality of Orphée's descent into hell, Œdipe's meeting with the Sphinx or Renaud's madness in the enchanted garden.

In many Expressionistic plays the settings seem to come alive. Objects become or seem to become animated. In Act II of *From Morn till Midnight* the set is dominated by a skeletal tree to which the hero speaks as if it were human. This is like Cocteau's theory "du décor qui bouge" or "moving settings." He speaks often of the universe as being guided by a malevolent intelligence. This is the theme of *La Machine infernale*. So, for example, Jocasta's scarf, with which she will ultimately hang herself, seems to plot her death. It catches on a branch, it tangles on the axle of a chariot. The whole universe is an infernal machine cocked and ready to explode.

These similarities are all traceable to common preoccupations: a focusing on certain rather haunted character types, the desire to adapt the methods of poetry to the stage, the author's wish to express his own subjectivity rather than to imitate an action, to reproduce life and people as they appear to the eye of common sense. Yet there are important differences, especially differences in tone and atmosphere, between the world of Cocteau and the world of the Expressionists. Cocteau's plays take place on a well-defined, well-lighted stage. The action is lit from all sides. There is nothing of the shadow world, so typical of Expressionism and much of the German tradition. Nietzsche's Zarathustra cries: "I am light. Oh! If I were night! Why am I not shadows and darkness!" The darkness of a Rembrandt painting, the shadow world of Jean Paul or Novalis, typify a certain kind of German mysticism. Strindberg's *Dream Play,* one of the seminal works of Expressionism, calls up a murky oneiric atmosphere.

Cocteau, on the contrary, has behind him a Descartes, a Racine, a Voltaire. The vestige of classical values is still present in his works, as in those of Gide. He does not penetrate as far as the Expressionists into the shadowy realms of subjectivity. Although the action of his plays is often obscure in meaning, the characters dialogue with all the self-assurance of Racine's characters, who know what they are and why they are. The darker realms remain beyond a border that is never crossed. Cocteau is a rationalist without a rationale; his reason destroys values rather than creating them; he places his characters in the world and then proceeds to make that world uninhabitable for them. Many of his deepest feelings about human nature are like those of the German Expressionists, but these feelings operate in a realm formed by the classics and under the pressure of values which he is powerless to ignore.

Cocteau denies the influence of most of the writers and the literary movements contemporaneous with himself. He has carefully selected the influences to which he will admit; he prefers to acknowledge them in another domain, painting or music, or among the dead—Radiguet. This is not merely because he is sensitive to criticism that he is a *pasticheur;* in point of fact, he has never been willing to make entirely his own the realm of experience and expression which Surrealism and Expressionism proposed to him. By a continual reflexive act, self-critical or self-protective, he withdraws from the modes of action of those very poets he himself had named as the exemplary masters of his generation—Rimbaud, Ducasse, Nerval, Sade.

Much of Cocteau's poetry, certain surreal fragments of *Opium* or *Potomak,* represent an effort to explore the deepest regions of the personality. And yet, in the last analysis, Cocteau refused to make this exploration, realizing perhaps that to do so might have taken him out of the realm of literature. Or perhaps he realized that certain dangers lay in delving too deeply within himself. Whereas Rimbaud abandoned poetry altogether partially for this reason—because he had gone too deeply into those regions of the soul where disease and madness mingle with the greatest lucidity—Cocteau merely retreated. He retreated toward the world of form and order represented by Maritain and the great classical tradition. Yet the retreat was an uneasy one. The characters he creates in his plays are at home in neither realm. Their malaise suggests an unresolved conflict, a struggle between the tradition of order and the forces of spiritual anarchy. Cocteau plays one off against the other and makes no commitment to either. He carefully maintains the integrity of his soul's disorder, but he does not explore it.

He explores instead in another direction. Insofar as we can identify Cocteau with any particular esthetic, it must be with the poetic idealism of Mallarmé. In Mallarmé syntactical compression, purposeful ambiguity, asyndeton, synecdoche, and such devices which tend to obscure the link between language and things, give us the impression of a purely phenomenal world where the mind intuits only itself. The world of moral obligation is left behind. Emotion, which always tends to attach man to the world of beings, is looked on as a distraction. The only emotion permissible is a kind of intellectual delectation, a lyrical excitement in the discovery of unexpected verbal and ideational relationships. It is related to the joy of the philosopher, but streamlined and intensified, operating under the pressure of formal principles rather than the necessities of a world of structured existents.

In Cocteau, as in Mallarmé, the metaphor is the locus of mind and reality. His poetry is always retreating from the world, tending toward some realm of pure abstraction. Cocteau's characters behave as if they themselves were pure poets. Their expressionism is chiefly limited to *one* realm of the Self. It is in this that Cocteau differs from the Surrealists and the German Expressionists. He was unwilling or unable to commit himself —and the characters of his plays—to the total and uncompromising kind of self-knowledge which is explosive and Dionysiac in nature. And, of course, pure poetry offers a convenient escape hatch from the classical tradition which demands commitment to a system of moral ideas and a code of behavior. Of all writers, the pure poets are the most uncommitted. Or we might say that they choose their commitment in a realm which does not make demands on the total personality.

And yet Cocteau's idealism is not identical with that of Mallarmé. He is not content with Mallarmé's brand of mystical contemplation—symbolized by the now famous swan frozen in the ice of a lake. Perhaps because of the very nature of his chosen medium, the drama, Cocteau is always trying somehow to get back to the world, to make commitment possible. Cocteau's "angelism," his "purity," are in contradiction with a contrary impulse toward the world with all its concrete solicitations. Cocteau is not, in the last analysis, a philosophical poet. He is not content to use poetry as a kind of supreme metaphysical game which, ultimately, has little significance beyond itself. No doubt it is impossible to write a "pure" drama; but another writer comes far closer to the purely metaphysical concern that we find in Mallarmé: Jean Giraudoux.

Despite the bewildering variety of allegiances, friendships and influences which his work and life display, Cocteau's dramas seem assignable to a specific realm of the theater. Since the end of the nineteenth century, French theater has tended to split into two main currents. The first of these, which has its source in the realism of the great nineteenth century novelists, is best represented by the famous renovator Antoine, founder of the Théâtre Libre. The other current goes back in a direct line to Romanticism and its most important descendant, Symbolism, thus showing a clear affiliation with expressionistic art and thought. It is represented in the theater by Lugné-Poë and the Théâtre de l'Œuvre et de l'Art. Cocteau is clearly in the second group, associated with such writers as Maeterlinck, Rostand and Giraudoux. Cocteau has written realistic plays. But his most original work evokes a strange world of poetry where characters move in obedience to the laws of a fantastic destiny. Cocteau and Giraudoux are the two main representatives of the *théâtre d'art.*[8]

In the works of both Giraudoux and Cocteau an ideal world is evoked, yet, by a deliberate irony, it is either impossible or futile to attain it. Giraudoux, as Mme Claude-Edmonde Magny tells us in her penetrating study, *Précieux Giraudoux,* is committed by his very syntax to a world of perfection.[9] Every character in his plays tends to assume the status of an Essence, or better, a Platonic Idea. In these plays, men seek to become like gods. Mme Magny traces this demiurgic movement to a fundamentally ambiguous conception of man's place in the universe. Giraudoux's characters repeatedly act out a movement toward and away from total purity. They revolt against being men, and they refuse to become gods.

Both Cocteau and Giraudoux question the nature of reality. Neither of them seems capable of assigning to man his definitive place in the universe. Their heroes aspire toward a dream of total purity and almost simultaneously reject it in favor of the familiar chaos of the world.

There is a strong Platonic strain to many of Cocteau's works, and especially to his statements about the nature and function of poetry. In *Le Mystère laic* (1928) he speaks of the poet as a kind of Platonist who attempts to capture a mysterious reality: "Poetry imitates a reality of which our world possesses only the intuition."[10] Like the Platonists, he associates this mystery with mathematics. The poem or play is a machine which captures the mystery of the universe by a kind of algebra: "The poet does not dream; he counts." "Poetry is nothing but figures, algebra, geometry, operations and proofs." "I fly by machine and I advance by falls." Poetic intuition is described as "immobile speed," or "velvet speed," in reference to the rapid associations which distinguish much of Cocteau's poetry. Poetry also displays the "short speed" of the slow motion camera, a comparison which seems at first thought contradictory to the preceding. But Cocteau is probably indicating here, in his typically metaphorical way, the fact that poetry produces one single, unified impression, which slowly moves and evolves, through the rapid projection of a great many images.[11]

The notion of poetry as machine is central to Cocteau's thought. It appears first in the use of gags, *trucs* and mechanical devices which constitute the spectacle of his early plays; it is inherent in the somewhat different spectacle reproduced by the mechanical eye of the motion picture camera. Most important of all is a metaphysical notion and use of poetry which aligns Cocteau with Mallarmé and Valéry. Indeed, the notion derives directly from Valéry, who has formulated the function of poetry thus: "In truth, a poem is a sort of machine for producing the poetic state by means of words." [12] It is chiefly in the later poems and plays of Cocteau that this conception of poetry becomes operative. Here we find Cocteau using incantation, in which words or phrases are repeated to give an effect of mechanical reiteration.[13] The incantation is designed to "capture" or subdue the mysterious "forces" in which the poet is immersed: "The poet is the vehicle, the natural medium of unknown forces which maneuver him, which profit by his purity to spread themselves through the world and, if not resolve, at least intensify to the point of nausea problems against which all wish to be on guard from the moment they wake up." [14] Here Cocteau seems to join the Platonism of Giraudoux. Through poetry we are able to make contact with the otherworld of ideas. Yet, like Giraudoux, Cocteau draws back before this world of ideas, feeling that to pursue the quest too far would perhaps endanger his own humanity.

The difference between Cocteau and Giraudoux lies chiefly in this: Giraudoux sees a metaphysical dilemma and organizes his dramas in terms of this dilemma. His characters emerge full-blown into a metaphysical war wherein the ranks are drawn and the plan of battle clearly devised. The characters are personified Essences; the metaphors posit some object or quality which represents the essentiality of a character. Hélène in *La Guerre de Troie n'aura pas lieu* is pure femininity. Lia in *Sodome et Gomorrhe* is pure humanity. One character is light, another darkness; one is earth, another fire. They function as ideas in a circular dialectic. Cocteau's fundamental motive is not philosophical, however. He is not rehearsing a philosophical problem.

Cocteau has said: "Poetry is a machine for making love." [15] The word he uses is *fabriquer,* not *faire,* and yet the suggestion of a pun is undeniable. Poetry is a form of seduction; it is used by Cocteau to win over and "charm" his readers. This is the most obvious explanation of the pun. Cocteau means something else too. The quotation is taken from his religious meditation, *Lettre à Jacques Maritain.* Poetry creates love as a kind of essence which has its own being and can be transmitted from one soul to another. It is like the Christian concept of grace: a hypostatic quality which exists spiritually in time and space. This, considering the context of the statement, is its intended meaning. Still a third meaning is possible, and as we examine Cocteau's works, we shall see it loom large.

Poetry may be used like love, perhaps even as a substitute for love. The universe, as Cocteau sees it, is full of terrible obstacles to the free operation of emotion, of love. These obstacles are human indifference, the cruelty of nature and the neurotic fears and inhibitions which we find within ourselves. Poetry is a weapon, perhaps the only weapon, capable of freeing the power of love. The characters of a Cocteau play are in the grip of an emotional—not a philosophical—dilemma, and they use poetry and the powerful ambiguities of metaphor accordingly.

Metaphor in Cocteau has a much less univocal function than in Giraudoux. His characters are divided as he himself is divided. They are all possible metaphors at one and the same time. His heroes long for and flee the world of commitment or love, just as they long to know themselves and do not dare to do so. The main impulse of Cocteau's work is psychological rather than metaphysical. His characters construct a universe to suit the needs of their own troubled psyches. It is an unsubstantial universe which changes as their needs and problems change. The general solution which Cocteau accepts is a kind of idealism; but it is only tentative, as, indeed, his constant experiments with form would suggest.

The motive behind Cocteau's work cannot be deduced from a study of influences. It is not the classical urge to imitate life and to instruct thereby, any more than it is the expressionistic impulse to use art as the supreme form of knowledge. Nor is it the philosophical-poetic impulse of Mallarmé and Giraudoux. Cocteau's alignment with the great wonder-workers of the *entre deux guerres* was always shifting and tentative; he ridiculed them, ridiculed himself, and made himself over from scratch each time he began a new work. He revised each program and tried to solve his own psychological and moral riddle with formulas that refused to work. But perhaps they did not work because he did not want them to. He wanted to prove that they were doomed to failure, and, in fact, that nothing would work, or that the only thing that would work was failure itself. He took up "mystery" like a heraldic emblem, a coat of arms, devising verbal and dramatic strategies which would prove that there was no way out of the dilemma—the answer to all problems was that there was no answer, the solution was no solution; mystery replied to itself.

Cocteau's writings sometimes give the impression of an oratorio, extending over two decades, with Gide at one end answering Sartre at the other, Maritain dialoguing with André Breton, Mallarmé quarreling with Ràymond Radiguet, and Edmond Rostand standing in the wings reciting Alexandrines. The dialogues go on and on, the music swells, the actors never tire. This, however, is a distortion, a falsification, due precisely to the external, historical perspective. There is another kind of structure in Cocteau's opus, there is true organicity; the actors are not Gide and Sartre and Maritain at all, but the *personae* of a solemn human and artistic drama, the drama not of literary history in the 1920's but of Cocteau himself.

Theater as parade

COCTEAU'S FIRST EXPERIENCE OF THE GLAMOR AND PRESTIGE OF the theater was the smell of his mother's perfume and the shimmering beauty of her dresses as she prepared to go out for an evening at the Comédie-Française or the Opéra. She *was* the theater. Her velvet was the velvet of the loges, her jewels the sparkling brilliance of the chandelier. Like Proust's Marcel, Jean dreamed of the day when he too would be able to watch the magical rites for which his mother prepared with such ceremony. And, while still a boy, he put together in imagination a fantastic play which derived from Grand Guignol and the Mass at his parish church, la Trinité. In the courtyard at 45 rue La Bruyère, Cocteau and René Rocher, who later became director of the Antoine and Vieux-Colombier theaters, built their own small theater, experimenting endlessly with fantastic settings and ingenious machines.

The impact of his first visits to the theater, where he saw *La Biche au bois* and *Le Tour du monde en 80 jours,* were to retain a unique importance for Cocteau, who has declared, in *Portraits-Souvenirs:* "And never will the dying lament of Tristan as he watches the sea replace in our heart the 'Twenty thousand banknotes for you, Captain, if we arrive this evening at Liverpool' of Philéas Fogg, nor will the settings of the Ballet Russe replace the enchanted snows where the Indian chief uncoupled the locomotive." [1]

The theater was first symbolized for Cocteau by the divine frivolity of his mother's dresses. It was this same mixture of the ephemeral and the beautiful that he found again in his first play, *Le Tour du monde en 80 jours*. And for a long time, the meaning of the theater was closely associated with what Cocteau calls "the intense forms of minor beauty," [2] all of which he has defended and celebrated.

For a time, Cocteau met with his friends and played jazz piano in a night club, the famous Bœuf sur le toit. He wrote ballets for Diaghilev and was closely associated with the Ballet Russe for a number of years. The Fratellini clowns performed in his ballet *Le Bœuf sur le toit*. And he actually rehabilitated and managed the boxer Al Brown, who was bantamweight champion of the world from 1929 to 1935.

The people whom Cocteau adores, whom he celebrates again and again, are the stars, the boxers, the clowns, the fashion mannequins, who represent a kind of popularized image of the poet. "Serge Lifar and Al Brown and Greta Garbo and all the stars of the stage, of the ring, of the spotlights and even the mannequins of a Chanel fashion show, mannequins like jockeys who are their own horses and perform in a paddock of mirrors: I told myself that they participate in an analogous enchantment, that they possess the secret resources of lightning and its awesome tricks, that the public suspects them as much as poets, that the crowd adores them, hates them and watches for their slightest misstep and that it is essential, in order to enjoy them, to cultivate and rediscover the childhood that poets prolong until death and that the grown-ups of the cities pride themselves on having lost." [3]

Cocteau has always been more at home in the theater, working with actors and technicians, than in the world of journalism or literary polemics. He himself is a performer and has acted in a number of his own plays and films: Mercutio in *Roméo et Juliette;* Heurtebise in the revival of *Orphée;* the narrator in *Œdipe-Roi, Le Sang d'un poète, La Belle et la bête.* Cocteau is drawn to this highly publicized but little known world because he finds in this fraternity of performers, whether they be anonymous or renowned, an image of his own condition. All manifestations of "beauté mineure"—including extravagant women, such as the Marchesa Casati or Anna de Noailles, the stars, "les monstres sacrés," such as Sarah Bernhardt, Isadora Duncan and Edouard de Max, the acrobat Barbette, Mistinguett, Chaplin, the wax statues of the musée Grévin, Nijinsky—all somehow share the destiny of the poet.

All the forms of "beauté mineure" demonstrate a tragic law. The styles of women's clothes, for example, are condemned to the brief existence of a butterfly. "Fashion [*la mode*] dies young, and its condemned aspect gives it nobility." The theater itself is the scene of a nightly execution. "I see the actor or actress exhaust himself for us and lose—like an animal fatally wounded by destiny—this pale blood of the boards, lose it and hold it in with full hands, hold it in and 'hold' until the final bow on which the curtain falls, each evening, like the guillotine." [4]

It is evident that much of the poetry which Cocteau finds in these things arises from analogies with death. Death appears in many forms and with many different meanings in Cocteau's works. Often death is not death at all but the symbol for something else, usually an unnamed psychic disaster, a childhood terror which cannot be quite understood or expelled. This terror appears in the later plays as a feeling of persecution.

Very early in his career, Cocteau tried to externalize this feeling of terror by identifying himself with the performing artist. From the wings, but with all the excitement of a participant, he watched Nijinsky make his spectacular leap in *Spectre de la Rose* or dance the lead in Cocteau's own ballet, his first, *Le Dieu bleu;* or Edouard de Max as Nero or in some other role from his tragic repertoire. When Cocteau speaks of his own vocation, poetry, he frequently borrows a metaphor from the world of "beauté mineure." He symbolizes the equilibrium of the poet by evoking a circus acrobat. The poet must operate on many different levels, must balance many contrary forces if he is to save himself from a fatal fall. The performer (whether an acrobat or a woman entering a cocktail lounge) is always in danger of losing the precarious balance which is the secret of his or her ability to awe the hostile public. Balance is one of the secrets of Cocteau's life and art. His whole career has been an attempt to translate this visual image of balance, which first attracted him at the Eldorado, the Palais de Glace, the Vaudeville or the Médrano, into a moral and metaphysical attitude. It is no wonder then that he feels such an affinity with those who make public show of this power.

The performer is very much like a child who wants to see how dangerously he can play without getting hurt—or without being punished. There is something of the exhibitionist in every performer, and this is not the least important reason for Cocteau's feeling of affinity with them. While he was still in his teens, the curly-headed prodigy of the salons, Cocteau was an exhibitionist. And in his early ballets and plays, he is still showing off, like the very dancers and performers who animated these works on the stage.

Because he is braving and challenging the public, there is a certain anxiety in everything that Cocteau does. This explains in part his hostility to and fear of the public. The little boy braving his mother, the bad student braving his teachers, becomes the performer braving his audiences, yet "charming" them too, doing everything in his power to keep them from turning their attention to someone else. He tries to keep the attention of his audience focused upon himself as a performer rather than upon the ultimate meaning of the work. Hence he is constantly short-circuiting the impact of the work, bringing us back, by some device or other, to the clever mind behind the show. The show is indeed a "parade," a procession of events which appear, one after the other, each sporting some little surprise, contributing to the gaiety and the carnival air. But they are discontinuous. They come and go; and when the last gay costume has disappeared, there is a lingering feeling of sadness in the heart of the spectator. Cocteau's early works are a parade of surprises. Their essence—like the nature of the man himself who was notorious for his spontaneous and unexpected behavior—lies in the use of spectacle. Indeed, his theatrical development began with a search for plastic rather than literary or dramatic values.

Cocteau defines the new type of theater he was trying to create as "the plastic expression of poetry." [5] The term "poésie du théâtre" is associated with Cocteau in the public mind, and it is understood that Cocteau, when he speaks of "poésie du théâtre," does not mean plays in verse.[6] This is one of Cocteau's central dogmas and must be interpreted differently at different phases of his career. If we judge from his early theatrical works, *Parade* and *Les Mariés de la Tour Eiffel,* Cocteau means that poetry is inherent in spectacle, in the plastic elements which, although they are suggested by the text, are really created by the director, actors and technicians. It would be easy to evoke the prejudice of the literary critic and banish these works which are not really plays at all, and whose beauty, like that of the very "beauté mineure" which they imitate, hangs by a thread. Yet, insofar as imagination can reconstruct them, *Parade* and *Les Mariés de la Tour Eiffel* seem neither tricky nor dated, as we might have expected. Rather, they are touching minor works which seem infallibly to hit their mark, achieving no more and no less than what was intended.

The ballet *Parade,* performed in 1917 and 1920, is Cocteau's first work for the theater. There is no text, merely scenic and choreographic notes and a number of articles, written in defense of *Parade* and subsequent to it. *Parade* is nevertheless a symbolic compression of much that was to come.

Cocteau tells us that the conclusive discovery of his own "manner" took place one night in 1912 when he was walking through the Place de la Concorde with Diaghilev and Nijinsky. Cocteau was trying to discover why Diaghilev was so reserved in his praises, and the latter, finally, adjusting his monocle, spoke the famous words: "Etonne-moi"—"Astonish me." And, Cocteau continues, the evening of the opening of *Parade* he did just that. Why was Diaghilev astonished by *Parade,* and what is the nature and importance of this now legendary ballet?

The first "scandal" associated with *Parade* concerns Picasso. Cocteau says that there was a virtual dictatorship by a clique of artists in Montparnasse and Montmartre. These artists, Picasso's friends and colleagues, were opposed to his becoming a mere scenic designer for the Ballet Russe. But Picasso accompanied Cocteau to Rome, and there, with the collaboration of several young Futurist painters, produced the set and costumes which were to elicit an outburst of fury from the Parisian public. The light, satirical music of Erik Satie was equally provoking. Yet now, at a distance of almost forty years, it is difficult to imagine why the spectators reached such a peak of fury that Guillaume Apollinaire, in his soldier's uniform, had to protect Picasso, Satie and Cocteau from a group of women armed with hatpins.

The plot of the ballet is simple. The stage represents a street-fair theater, or *théâtre forain,* somewhere in Paris. Three music hall numbers—by a Chinese Juggler, Acrobats and a Little American Girl—are performed in front of the theater. Then, three gesticulating Managers attempt to convince the crowd to go inside for the whole show. But no one goes in, and finally the Managers fall, exhausted. Again the performers appear and try to convince the crowd that "the show is on the inside."

Cocteau asserts that Picasso and Satie, whose contributions to *Parade* caused most of the uproar, were his only Masters. Like many of Cocteau's assertions, this must be taken with a grain of salt. The expression of his debt to a painter and a composer may be a means of dispensing himself from other debts, to Rostand or Gide for example, which he feels less inclined to mention. Satie, Diaghilev, Picasso, Radiguet and the others all told Cocteau what he wanted to hear. No doubt, even if he had never known them, Cocteau would have followed much the same path.[7]

Cocteau learned from Picasso what he calls the "Picassian method." It is basically a restatement of one of the precepts of the *esprit nouveau* and consists in the careful distortion of observed reality. Hence, *Parade* was called a "realistic" ballet. The Little American Girl, for example, rides a bicycle, imitates Charlie Chaplin and takes a snapshot. This kind of detail is the "parade" which must be enhanced by the artist's vision, which alone can take us "on the inside." Whatever else *Parade* may have been, it was above all a series of visual surprises, for Cocteau was collaborating with the greatest modern master of sight gags. The early works of Cocteau are not devoid of a certain intention to scandalize or *épater le bourgeois*. The adaptation of Picasso's vivid and often comic vision to the choreography of a ballet accomplishes that, at the expense, perhaps, of other and more conventional goals.

Les Mariés de la Tour Eiffel, produced in 1921, is the first of his works which, Cocteau believed, was not derivative: "Until *Les Mariés de la Tour Eiffel,* the first work in which I owe nothing to anyone, which resembles no other work, where I found my formula, I forced the lock and twisted my key in all directions." [8] (The resemblance between *Les Mariés* and *Les Mamelles de Tirésias* by Apollinaire need not necessarily imply imitation. *Un Chapeau de paille d'Italie* by Labiche, produced originally in 1851 and revived many times in succeeding years, is also a forerunner of *Les Mariés.*)

The action of *Les Mariés de la Tour Eiffel* unrolls to the music of the famous Six: Auric, Milhaud, Poulenc, Tailleferre and Honegger (Louis Durey was not represented). The characters do not speak. Instead, there are two narrators, costumed as phonographs, who recite the parts which the actors pantomime, and comment on the events which take place. The action takes place on the first platform of the Eiffel Tower and begins with the arrival of a wedding party, the members of which march in like dogs walking on their hind legs in a circus act. The two phonographs announce them: "The bride, gentle as a lamb." "The father-in-law, rich as Crœsus." "The groom, handsome as a heart." "The mother-in-law, false as a bad penny." "The general, stupid as a goose." "The men of honor, strong as Turks." "The maids of honor, fresh as roses." [9]

The satirical intention, carried through in the music, becomes clearer as the farce proceeds. The marriage party represents the banal world of daily life. On the other hand, the photographer, with his surprising camera from which an ostrich, a child, a lion and a bathing beauty emerge, represents the marvelous. The two worlds are reconciled (at least to the eye) when, at the end of the play, the members of the wedding party disappear one by one into the camera.

The phonographs speak for the actors in the way that a sophisticated person repeats an amusing conversation, bringing out the gaucheries and the vulgarisms which might normally pass unnoticed. The actors move like puppets, satirizing themselves. The disconcerting camera constantly throws the actors into a new round of excitement as the farce develops with the spontaneity of a folk dance. Indeed, Cocteau tells us that in *Les Mariés,* especially in the musical score, popular and folk art provided much of the inspiration: "In *Les Mariés* we employ the popular resources which France despises at home but approves abroad when a French or foreign musician exploits them." [10]

The play is set in motion when the hunter—who is pursuing the ostrich which has escaped from the photographer's camera —shoots, not the ostrich, but a large blue message which announces the arrival of the wedding procession. The message flutters to earth like a wounded bird, and the director of the Eiffel Tower prepares to receive the guests. The visual playfulness of all this is evident. And this is only the beginning. There is the bathing beauty who does a dance, the lion who devours the general. Both emerge from and return into the camera.

How are these fantasies given an organic link with the play as a whole? The fact that they are all elements of a general satirical intention is part of the answer. But further, Cocteau is trying to awaken in us a sense of the marvelous. He is saying that dance and gesture are in themselves a kind of moral attitude, and that the absurdity of bourgeois life must be relieved by poetry and this sense of the marvelous or fantastic. Even a commonplace lunch on the Eiffel Tower can become a ballet, can be lifted, that is, to the dignity and mystery of art.

If this is indeed art, we might ask: Art on what level and with how much dignity? The text of the play is very brief and its meaning not altogether clear, as Cocteau seems to say when he appropriates to himself the words of the photographer: "Since these mysteries surpass us, let us pretend to be their organizer." [11] This is an art of spectacle, and we cannot expect much meaning, plot or other forms of dramatic logic. The search for structure and meaning in the dramatic form is Cocteau's most persistent problem, and he resolved it differently, and with varying degrees of success, at different stages of his career.

Perhaps because he was still so close to the Ballet Russe, still preoccupied with the scenic rather than the literary aspects of playwriting, Cocteau was content to write a play without any real central theme or concern. Cocteau has often said that he developed late—"I am not in childhood, but almost. My childhood is interminable" [12]—and this observation is confirmed by his development as a playwright. In *Parade* and *Les Mariés,* he is an ingenious child showing off a thousand tricks. The real unity of *Les Mariés* is not in meaning but in spectacle: in the music, the dances, the masks, the pantomimes, which resolve contradictions on the literary level by immersing them in the continuity of a dance. Again, as in *Parade,* performance is an essential element. It is therefore irrelevant to confront these bare, brief texts without re-creating, at least in imagination, the splendid productions in which they came to life.

A summary of Cocteau's early works should include *Le Bœuf sur le toit,* a pantomime-ballet, produced in 1920 with music by Darius Milhaud, scenery by Raoul Dufy, and performed by the famous Fratellini clowns of the Cirque Médrano. The actors wear huge papier-mâché heads, a favorite device of Cocteau's. The grotesque paper sculptures dehumanize the actors, who, in their performance, carry out this intention: They are "settings which move." They are dehumanized because they represent the New York of speak-easies and the jazz age which it was the

Paris rage to imitate after the first war. Cocteau speaks disparagingly of this fad: "It is needless to add that the cult of New York, the present-day estheticism, seems to me just as depressing as the cult of Venice." [13] Undoubtedly, though, Cocteau contributed as much as anyone to making it fashionable.

The little drama takes place in a speak-easy. It shows the same visual inventiveness, the same ability to utilize the *trouvailles* of the set or the actors, as *Parade* and *Les Mariés*. A boxer, a Negro dwarf, two women and a bookie are in a bar—billiards, dice game, coquetry. They are raided by the police, but the bartender saves the day by lowering the rotating electric fan, which decapitates the policeman. Then one of the women dances triumphantly—on her hands—like the Salome of the cathedral of Rouen. In the finale, the bartender revives the policeman, restores his head to him, and for this service, presents him with a bill three yards long.

Cocteau modestly suggests that the success of this little piece was an indication of the poor taste of the Parisian public. The jazz age in America, if it was a form of adolescent rebellion and middle-aged self-indulgence, was nevertheless an authentic expression of American culture. Reinterpreted by French Bohemians and dilettantes, it could be no more than night club entertainment. *Le Bœuf sur le toit,* however, anticipated the fad and testifies to Cocteau's ability to guess which way the public would jump. At this point, Cocteau seems to have been still too concerned with the public (although disparaging it), too responsive to it, too much a part of it. This unfortunate tendency to play to the grandstand has never altogether disappeared from his work.

The last of Cocteau's "spectacle" plays is *Roméo et Juliette,* a free adaptation of Shakespeare, written in 1916 and produced in 1924. The play was directed by Cocteau, who played the role of Mercutio.

In *Roméo et Juliette,* Cocteau follows the same procedure, if somewhat less drastically, as in his adaptations of Sophocles. The verbal dimension, the "poetry" of Shakespeare, is reduced to a minimum. Note for example, Romeo's famous discovery of Juliet (Act I, scene 5):

O, she doth teach the torches to burn bright!
It seems she hangs upon the cheek of night
Like a rich jewel in an Ethiop's ear;
Beauty too rich for use, for earth too dear!
So shines a snow-white swan trooping with crows,
As this fair lady o'er her fellows shows.
The measure done, I'll watch her place of stand,
And, touching hers, make blessed my rude hand.
Did my heart love till now? forswear it, sight!
I never saw true beauty till this night.

This speech is reduced to three lines:

Je n'avais jamais aimé. Un seul diamant orne l'oreille de la nuit, c'est elle. A quoi servent ces lustres ridicules?

Even more drastic is the treatment of the balcony scene:

> Il se moque de l'amour, celui qui n'a jamais ressenti l'amour. (*Juliette paraît à la fenêtre, sa main pend et se balance.*) Oh! Juliette, c'est elle! Si elle savait. On dirait qu'elle parle— Non — quand elle sort, c'est le soleil et tous les oiseaux chantent. Voilà qu'elle pose sa joue contre sa main. Je voudrais être son petit gant. (Act II, scene 1)

Almost no attempt is made to reproduce Shakespearian lyricism. The comic scenes are almost entirely done away with; for example, the sad buffoonery of Peter and the musicians after the mock death of Juliet (Act IV, scene 5). The speeches of Mercutio are very much shortened. Frequently, there is a clear loss of dramatic irony or of character revelation as, for instance, in Act I, scene 2, where Romeo befuddles the Capulet servingman by pretending that he cannot read. Cocteau has not struggled with the problem of translation. He has simply ignored it. We are left with the skeleton of a play which it becomes the responsibility of the director and the actors to animate. (And, of course, Cocteau was both during the play's brief run.)

The scenic notes which are included in the published text of *Roméo et Juliette* give some indication of the general nature of the performance and a clue to Cocteau's description of the play as a pretext for a choreographic production, or *mise en scène choréographique.*[14]

The prologue is spoken by an actor who, as the result of an optical illusion, appears to fly. The settings are mobile, and the streets and courtyards are formed, by the moving flats, as the action requires. Roméo, alone of all the young men of Verona, does not wear a sword, and he walks like a somnambulist. Here, for the first time, appears the technique which Cocteau later used with such success in his ballet *Le Jeune homme et la mort*. The movements of Benvolio and Roméo (Act I, scene 2) have been harmonized with a dance rhythm that is not played during performance. They move to an absent music—one of the choreographic aspects of the production. A servant leaves the stage running in slow motion through the perspectives of the set. The actors may speak with their backs to the public as, for example, does Capulet at the feast scene (Act I, scene 5). Juliette discovers Roméo's identity not at the feast but afterwards, watching from her bedroom window, as the nurse unhooks her dress. The prologue to Act II is spoken by a compound figure formed of two actors, the aim being to give very wide gestures. Drum roll after each line. When Mercutio is fatally wounded by Tybalt, a stagehand comes on stage and mysteriously carries off Mercutio's sword. When Tybalt, a moment later, is wounded by Roméo, he grasps the latter's ankle in a death grip. Benvolio must unclasp the dead fingers before Roméo is able to flee.

One detail, which we find Cocteau using in later works, is indicated in Shakespeare's text. Roméo throws himself on the floor like a child in a tantrum. Later, Juliette lies on her stomach to talk to Roméo over the edge of the balcony. And, at the end of this same scene, Juliette throws a tantrum, face down on the floor. The time change, after Juliette's mock death, is suggested by a long band of black material which the stage-hands unroll in front of the deathbed. When they disappear, the night has become morning. In the last act, the apothecary's shop is actually carried onstage, with the apothecary concealed behind it, while Roméo walks in the streets of Mantua.

These are some of the details by which Cocteau sought to achieve a visual counterpart of Shakespearian lyricism. But to judge the production, we should have to know how the role of Roméo was interpreted, if the quality of impetuous and soaring imagination, so typical of the Shakespearian hero, was achieved in spite of an abbreviated text. And did Juliette have that lucid tenderness which makes her such an appealing heroine? Unfortunately, the production was given only a limited number of times in 1924 at the Soirées de Paris. The production details with which we are supplied do not seem to indicate a real interpretation of the text. They are for the eye alone. The stylization of a play is too easy a means for achieving form. Dances, masks and mobile sets do not provide that definitive sense of interpretation and commentary which it is the job of the production to add to the written text.

Cocteau has performed a neat job of surgery on Shakespeare's lyricism; in its place he has given us "poésie du théâtre" in its most material form, that is, the parade, the spectacle, the imitation of minor beauty. For the lyrical dimension Cocteau substitutes a poetry of devices, *trucs,* to use the French expression. This is, once again, the dependence on spectacle. Cocteau has attempted to defend the poetry of the *trucs,* an issue on which he has been much attacked, with statements very reminiscent of his theory of poetry as machine: "The *truc* is art itself." "Poetry is a vast pun." [15]

In these statements, Cocteau appears to be expressing rather intuitively an idea which modern critics have rendered respectable. The essence of the pun is ambiguity: two meanings arising from a single word or phrase. The same is true of the metaphor. It is an image which is used with a double sense. It denotes one thing and connotes another. Poetry arises out of the tension between the two meanings. The poem itself is a pun in that it "stands for" more than it is. The whole is more than a mere total of words or images. From it the imagination leaps out along radii of complementary meanings to a deeply felt truth. The poem, like a pun, has a second meaning which appears unexpectedly amidst the structure of familiar counters.

But the fact of the matter is that Cocteau is reversing the process. He is not merely trying to justify the complexities of poetry by reference to a simple linguistic phenomenon, the pun. He is trying to justify his puns by reference to the complexities of poetry. A pun is only a pun; and the *trucs* of Cocteau's early works cannot be dignified with the name of poetry.

This unjustifiable reversal is made clear in a passage of *Le Rappel à l'ordre*: ". . . the painter and the musician must not use the spectacle of machines to mechanize their art, but must use instead the measured exaltation which the spectacle of machines causes in order to express an object wholly different and more intimate." [16] Let us assume here that Cocteau means not only machines, in the literal sense, as they are found in the paintings of Fernand Léger, but also devices, such as we find in Cocteau's own poems and plays. This interpretation is justified by his explicit description of poetry as a kind of verbal machine. Then it would appear that Cocteau is defending devices in and for themselves—provided of course that they suggest something beyond themselves, are a projection of some psychological or spiritual mechanism. While a device or *truc* may conceivably function poetically, such tricks as the revolving fan of *Le Bœuf sur le toit* or the camera of *Les Mariés* can be justified only in terms of an esthetic which makes spectacle the prime value.

These quotations merely confirm our observations of Cocteau's early works; and they indicate the direction of his future development. As we shall see, in *Orphée,* Cocteau attempted to make his devices less autonomous, to incorporate them in the texture and meaning of his works as an organic whole. At this stage of his career, Cocteau had not yet fully merged spectacle and meaning. From the beginning, he had an astonishing dexterity in the discovery and use of effects. But his literary development, which implies the intellectual and the moral, was a much slower and more painful process.

Dream and discontinuity

THE BASIC DIVERSITY OF FILM AND STAGE MAKES IT IMPOSSIBLE, in this study of Cocteau's theater, to treat his films at length. Yet these films represent a revision and extension of his general esthetic of the theater; indeed, in Cocteau's major films we have a fuller justification of the esthetic of parade than in the early stage works themselves.

Spectacle, which is never entirely absent from the works of Cocteau, reaches its full importance in the films, where the *truc* is raised to a higher power by the very nature of the film medium. Again there is the parade, the dream float of images, the qualitative progression of autonomous inventions piled one on another, merging in endless metamorphoses. Yet as film images, rather than the finite *trucs* of the stage, they achieve a special degree of "poésie du théâtre" and vibrate with symbolic power. The nature of Cocteau's film poetry is defined in *Le Sang d'un poète* (1932).

Le Sang d'un poète begins with the following words, which underline the film's mystery, projected upon the screen: "Every poem is a blazon that must be deciphered." The film is further defined as "a realistic documentary of unreal events." And finally "the author dedicates this reel of allegories to the memory of Pisanello, Paolo Uccello, Piero della Francesca, Andrea del Castagno, painters of blazons and enigmas." The film proper begins with the shot of a crumbling smokestack, which is again seen disintegrating at the end of the film.[1]

The first episode is entitled "The Wounded Hand or the Scars of the Poet." The poet is now seen in his studio. He is naked from the waist up; on his head is a wig in the style of the period of Louis XV. This wig, as well as the costumes of other characters and a conspicuously placed statue of Diderot in a subsequent episode, suggests that the poet, as wonder-worker and magician, is in conflict with his skeptical and rationalistic age. The eighteenth century, the Age of Reason, produced no significant poets. There is, however, no historical location in the film; the time is at once any time and the present.

The poet is standing in front of an easel on which he has drawn a face with a living mouth. The poet rubs off the mouth; goes to the door to admit a friend; the friend, in Louis XV

costume, turns away with horror. The mouth has been transferred to the poet's hand. After futile efforts to eradicate the
mouth, the poet caresses his body, apparently reaches an orgasm
and falls asleep.

The next morning the poet rubs the mouth off his hand onto
the face of a life-size statue which represents a woman. The second episode then follows. It is entitled "Do the Walls Have
Ears?"

The statue says to the poet: "Do you think that it is so simple
to rid yourself of a wound, to close the mouth of a wound?"
While the statue is speaking, the camera reveals that the door
and windows have disappeared. The only way out of the room
is the mirror, through which the poet finally plunges.

The second episode takes place chiefly in the realm beyond
the mirror, where the poet moves with difficulty as if in a
dream. He is in a hotel corridor, L'Hôtel des Folies-Dra-
matiques; since art holds the mirror up to nature, this is undoubtedly the world of art. The name of the hotel, however,
suggests that this is the art of music hall and night club, the
vulgar art of "beauté mineure." Here, the poet now becomes
a voyeur, peeks through a series of four keyholes and observes
a series of events of a mysterious nature.

The poet approaches the first door in the corridor and peers
through the keyhole. He sees an execution in progress; a
Mexican, who strongly resembles the poet, is fired on; he falls,
then mysteriously rises; he is shot, falls, and rises again.

The poet now approaches the second door, on which is a sign
reading "Leçons de Vol." Within, a cruel old woman with a

whip is teaching a little girl to fly. The scene is reminiscent of the one in *Oliver Twist* where Fagin teaches the children to steal; hence it is evident that the sign means both "Flying Lessons" and "Lessons in Theft." Finally the little girl flys to the ceiling, where she sticks out her tongue at her teacher.

The poet moves with extreme difficulty, as if through a strange resistant medium, to the third door. The voice of the narrator says: "The mysteries of China." The poet tears a wad of paper out of the keyhole and looks into the room, where he sees an opium pipe and smoke rising from it. As he maneuvers himself, to see more clearly, an eye looks out of the keyhole, back at him.

He now approaches the fourth door, in front of which, side by side, stand two shoes—a man's and a woman's. The narrator says: "In room nineteen the Hermaphrodite held desperate rendez-vous." Peering through the keyhole, the poet sees a long divan. A white face appears above the divan while an endless spiral turns. There is a roll of drums and a woman's body now appears, drawn below the face. Next, as the drums roll again, a man's leg and arm appear through the drawing. The poet strains to see, his back creasing in a sensual way. After other limbs have appeared on the couch, the hand lifts a covering at the loins, and there appears a sign which reads "Danger of death."

Once again at the third door the poet witnesses a confused scene—a mask wearing a wig, arms and legs on a woman's body, scattered clothing—and hears the whispering of lovers.

The poet goes on to the end of the hall. There, a woman's

hand offers him a pistol. She recites, like a salesgirl reading instructions on a package, "Instructions. Grip the pistol firmly. Release the safety catch. Cock the pistol. Place the index finger on the trigger. Place the barrel against the temple. Fire." The poet, lit by brilliant arc-lights, appears with blood running from his temple, a crown of laurel on his head. The narrator says ironically: "Always for glory!" The poet curses under his breath.

Like a man pursued, the poet now tries to return. Still living, he is expelled from the mirror to the singing of a choir of children. Taking a mallet, he proceeds to demolish the statue. In the process he becomes covered with dust and debris. The voice of the narrator announces: "In breaking statues one risks becoming one oneself."

The next episode begins with the poet, now a statue, being demolished by a group of schoolboys. This episode is called "The Snowball Fight" and takes place in the cité Monthiers, a small square below Montmartre, where Cocteau often played as a boy. This is presumably a flashback and shows how the poet acquired the wound which he now bears. The same scene has been described in *Les Enfants terribles* and appears in the film based on that novel.

The poet's wound is inflicted by Dargelos, the "cock of the college," a young tough about fourteen years old. Dargelos throws a snowball at his friend—who is, of course, the poet as a boy—and this treachery, not the snowball itself, causes the boy to fall, bleeding from the mouth. The other boys run away, leaving the body of their comrade in the snow.

The fourth episode, "The Profanation of the Host," takes its title from the painting by Paolo Uccello. We see the poet seated at a card-table, opposite the statue, which has become a living woman. The windows of the apartments surrounding the square have been turned into the loges of a theater where elegant men and women, dressed to the teeth, make small talk while waiting for the play to continue. One of the spectators is Barbette, the acrobat, costumed as a woman.

The poet is gambling his fate against the beautiful woman. The friend of the first episode, costumed and posed like Watteau's *L'Indifférent,* idly watches the game. At the poet's feet, in the snow, we see the body of the dead boy. The poet reaches under the table and steals the ace of hearts from the boy's cloak. A door opens at the head of a staircase, and the child's guardian angel, a half-naked Negro, descends the stairs. He wears wire wings and limps on one leg. Nearing the card-players, he covers the child's body with a cloak and lies upon it, to the accompaniment of a noise like the motor of an airplane. He strains with tremendous effort as he "absorbs" the child's body. Then he takes the ace of hearts back from the poet and returns up the stairs.

The woman says scornfully to the poet: "If you don't have the ace of hearts, darling, you're a goner." The poet's heart beats furiously. Slowly he takes a pistol from his pocket, raises it to his temple, fires. He falls under the table, bleeding, covered with snow while the spectators applaud. The woman once again becomes the statue of the first episode.

The final sequences of the film show the woman, become a living statue, moving into a celestial realm with a bull whose back is covered by a map of Europe. She is Europa, ravished by Jove in the shape of a bull. Art is divinized. The bull's horns become a lyre, and the woman is transformed into an emblematic abstraction, the work of art as posterity sees it, distant, precise, finally made clear if not understandable. The human drama out of which it grew is now distant and lost; only the emblem remains, the constellation of images, the symbol, but a symbol which is mysterious even though its outlines are finally clear. The narrator says: "Mortal boredom of immortality."

Cocteau himself has repeatedly refused to explain *Le Sang d'un poète*. The most illuminating exegesis which has been done on the film is that of C. G. Wallis. Mr. Wallis finds many unities in the film, which he analyzes by techniques we are more accustomed to see used on lyric poetry or novels, works of dense verbal texture. He attempts to unify the film by drawing threads of meaning out of its metaphors, finding an emblematic and analogical rather than a narrative and thematic unity. Since he is looking for something more than what he calls "unities of rhetoric and decoration," [2] he further tries to reduce these disparate allegories to philosophical categories. However, unity in the sense in which Mr. Wallis would find it in Cocteau is something that this poet is not especially concerned with. Cocteau himself says in the preface to the scenario of *Le Sang d'un poète:* "I searched for only the relief and the detail of images arising from the great night of the human body. I then immediately adopted them as the documentary scenes of another realm. That is why this film which possesses a single style . . . presents a multiple surface to exegesis. Its exegeses were innumerable. When asked about one of them, I always found it difficult to answer." [3] Mr. Wallis is in the predicament of the rationalistic critic who faces an irrational text; the unity of style and even the unity consequent on the single subject line are not sufficient to bear the weight of a structuring analysis.

Two lines of interpretation are possible. Mr. Wallis assumes an esthetic and philosophical unity in the film and attempts to relate part to part in terms of a central theme—the poet's discovery of the meaning of art. Because this art is hierophantic and occult, the use of allegory and symbol are justified. Mr. Wallis sees a development from "naïve" poet to "depersonalized" poet—from art as the simple representation of reality, in the sketch or life-drawing in episode one, to the final abnegation before art, the poet's suicide in the last episode.

In each episode, as Mr. Wallis points out, there are represented the philosophical categories of agent and patient: the painter and the sketch, the painter and the statue, the Mexican and the firing squad, the schoolmistress and the child, Dargelos and his buddy, and so on. The poet is agent vis à vis the work of art, yet he must also submit to his art, be victimized by it, as patient to agent; he must allow his art to use him to express itself.

The second line of interpretation might well start from a consideration of the film's style, that occult style which Mr.

Wallis justifies in terms of theme. The obscurities of the entire film suggest a close relationship with the disguises of dream. Freudian analysis postulates concealment, in this case allegory and symbol, and a limited number of sexual motivations. Further, the suffering or *patientia* which Mr. Wallis finds in the film is emotional rather than philosophical in quality. Finally, such an analysis has the added advantage of aiming at an irrational rather than a logical unity such as that required by the method of Mr. Wallis. And the very nature of the film medium, its close link with dreams and the unconscious, confirms the relevance of an interpretation which sees the film primarily as a psychological drama which attains only rarely to the total coherence of a play or a novel.

The question to be asked in regard to the film is less the esthetic question of the nature of art than its psychological corollary: What is the reason for such a conception of art? Why is the poet doomed to suffer, and why must his art be paid for with blood?

The fact that even the naïve art of a life-drawing has daemonic power is demonstrated by the mouth which appears on the sketch. This suggests that art is used as a substitute for some powerful sexual urge. As Mr. Wallis puts it, "the development of the power of poetry to a daemonic state within him was an erotic substitute for the loss of love." [4] The caresses which the poet applies to his own body, with the mouth transferred from sketch to hand, bear out this conclusion. All the forms of art which appear in the film are disguises of sexuality. The mouth represents sexuality conceived of as a dis-

figurement with no hope of reparation. The hopelessness of
the poet's sexual plight is represented by the absence of doors
and windows in the room when the poet awakes the morning
after his discovery of the narcissistic pleasure of art. The poet
is forced to escape from the room through the mirror. The
only cure for the psychic wound is through the creation of an
image world, a world wherein the pain of the wound can be
appeased by symbolic gratification, through art represented
by the mirror.

The second episode might be considered, at least in part, as
the search for the subject matter of poetry. All of these images—
the executed Mexican, the little girl who learns to fly, the opium
pipe, the hermaphrodite—are extremely obscure; they are vistas
of unknown worlds, the worlds of other men's lives, glimpsed
through the keyhole of a hotel room. These scenes are not to
be taken literally as the subject of poetry; they represent the
poetry of everyday life, the ordinary life of a dreary hotel,
which if we could only look through the keyhole would seem
as strange and compelling as an execution at dawn. Behind
the dull parade of life, although we see it only in brief glimpses,
lie beauty and terror.

The above considerations, however, in no way exhaust the
emotional or psychological component of the episode. It is
clear that the poet has become a voyeur, one who studies the
sexual behavior of other men, women and children. The curi-
osity which makes him peer through the keyhole is by no means
purely esthetic. He identifies himself with each scene that he
watches, apparently each time with the hope that the behavior

of other people will give him some clue to his own predicament, show him some way to solve his own sexual anomaly. However, he observes that all people are victims. Each one is confined to his own moral and emotional universe, represented by the walls of the hotel rooms in which the events take place. It may be also that he sees in opium and abnormal love a justification for his own form of substitute gratification, that is, art. These scenes all combine the real and the unreal, the human body and mechanical devices, which might be taken to indicate the compulsive, hence mechanical motive behind the characters' apparent humanity.

Such an analysis of this obscure episode, while tentative, at least has the merit of involving it more completely in the emotional climate of the film than does Mr. Wallis' ingenious treatment of it as representation of four aspects of dramatic poetry—the peripety of tragedy, mystery, sublimity, confusion between art and reality.

The poet's mock suicide at the end of the hotel corridor might be considered to terminate the first phase of the film, which shows the naïve poet, still drawing from life and interested in other men's lives. True art requires greater esthetic distance, greater symbolization. On emerging from the mirror the poet attempts to break the statue, that is, to deny the daemonic power of art and his own vocation. However, nothing can be changed; in destroying the statue, he becomes one himself. Mr. Wallis interprets this transformation ironically by suggesting that the statue represents the classic past, and that when the poet becomes a mere statue in the public square, we are seeing the solidification of the ego which is observed in conventional art from which daemonic genius is lacking. However, the transformation might just as well represent the transfiguration of the poet, his deification and historical apotheosis. The change is similar to the poet's more symbolical transformation at the end of the last episode, wherein he dies, leaving his work behind as a final testament.

The third episode, "The Snowball Fight," both describes the nature of the poet's wound, in more literal fashion, and postulates the wound's possible origin. The wound inflicted by Dargelos might represent no more than an act of treachery, betrayal by someone whom the boy loved, or it might equal an overt homosexual experience. At any rate, it is presented as a crucial trauma, with a determining effect on the poet's future life.

A purely psychological reading of the next episode, however hermetic, is not difficult. The poet cannot win in the game of love with the woman because his heart is already wounded by Dargelos, that is, committed to an intense and unchanging childhood version of love. The angel, who is perhaps a reincarnation of the "angel" Dargelos, "absorbs" the boy by a convincing imitation of the sexual act. The angel's claims to the boy are those of traumatic childhood experiences from which the adult is never wholly free; this creature is an allegorical representation of the fears and inhibitions which prevent the poet from being a true man, that is, a man who can love a woman. He is only a man qua poet; the link between art and homosexuality is thus clearly established.

The film suggests that it is attachment to the first love, Dargelos, which makes love of a woman impossible. There is no suggestion of the psychoanalytic explanation which places the cause of homosexuality in a too intense relationship with the mother; pederasty is the consequence of identification with the loved mother who herself loved a little boy.

Looked at in this way, the episode appears as a more highly detailed retelling of the scene in which the mouth (the wound) is transferred to the poet's hand. What was first presented in a compressed, emblematic form is now repeated in the form of a narrative. Both episodes convey a feeling of anxiety and terror, the blind struggle of a man trapped by his own psyche. The poet's attempt to wash off the wound in the first scene is identical, in emotional content, with the poet's terror as he sees he is going to lose the game of cards, the game of heterosexual love.

This time, in contrast to the earlier episode, the poet's suicide has the polish and precision of a work of art; and it takes place in a theater before applauding spectators. The poet destroys himself by his total submission to the work of art, and yet, paradoxically, art is intimately linked with biography—it is always the repetition of the mortal drama of childhood. Cocteau's film itself would serve to prove this rule. Since the poet has lost the ace of hearts, has tried to disguise his deepest childhood feelings and thus "profaned" the host or sacrament, he loses the game.

The poet's second death is a real death, contrasted to the first, which took place behind the mirror. The poet's death leaves only his creation, his true Self, as an enigma which the vulgar crowd applauds but does not understand. This death is symbolic as well as real, however; it represents the artist's death to the life of ordinary men and women as well as his abnegation of Self in creation. These versions of death, represented in allegorical fashion, are simultaneously and equally real.

The film ends with the crumbling chimney. The repetition of this image suggests the instantaneousness of the work of art as a spiritual event, outside of time; its images, which are necessarily concrete, material, temporal, are the representation of the timeless drama of the spirit. Time, incorporated in the events of the poet's youth until the final apotheosis of his creation, is no more than illusion or appearance. The truth of the poem is instantaneous and eternal, out of time, although it takes its hard-bought validity from a temporal drama.

Time is a persistent preoccupation with Cocteau and in *Journal d'un inconnu,* twenty-one years after *Le Sang d'un poète,* he develops some very dense paradoxes on this subject. In particular the chapter called "About Distances" revolves on the question of spatial and temporal relativity; Cocteau attempts to treat space and time phenomenologically, as constructed by the mind, in opposition to classical realistic notions. This chapter, written long after his major works, codifies their inherent idealism; the Self creates the world and cannot escape from its own limits or do more than question its illusions.

The film accents the mingling of art and life rather than their separation; barriers are broken down; categories dissolve in the chemistry of a dream. But a philosophical problem cannot exist in a dream where there is neither reason nor freedom; and it is precisely the dream, the dream technique, which triumphs in the film. A dream, to return to one of our central metaphors, is a parade of images, a qualitative progression. The dream play or film does not attempt to produce anything like the classical dramatic structure of Purpose, Passion and Perception. It is based on a "logic" of irrationality. The astonishing and unforgettable images of Cocteau's film do not form a truly dramatic development; but the film is less an art of logic or even plot than an art of images. The deepest poetry of the film lies in the use of images, and Cocteau is a master of film metaphor.

Cocteau had said that poetry was a machine; but with *Le Sang d'un poète,* he reversed the equation and proved that a machine was poetry. The film, like the poem, is a work of great compression; on a film lasting ninety minutes, the camera unfolds before us effects, and what Valéry would call "problems," which have taken months and sometimes years to formulate and solve. The camera, like the poem, is not limited by time or space; the abolition of these normal categories of human experience places the film in that phenomenal world where things are as we wish them or imagine them to be. Film images, however, are pictures rather than words; because of this fact, the film cannot achieve the same degree of logical unity as an art whose very medium is itself a form of abstraction from reality. The visible film image multiplies its associations past the point of control; its images are discontinuous.

Cocteau has recognized this inherent quality of the film image, and in his *Entretiens autour du cinématographe* he insists on it. Each image must be set off from the other, must not flow into the next. The discontinuous nature of film images thus points to the now generally accepted characterization of the film as being, in the words of Susanne Langer, in the "dream mode."

Mrs. Langer adduces chiefly the immediacy of the film in support of her theory. The spectator of a motion picture sees and hears with the camera, which is always at the center of events, creating "an eternal and ubiquitous virtual present." [5] This would seem to be so—to enlarge somewhat on Mrs. Langer —because the film reproduces the world of the imagination, the fantasy world where images flow unceasingly, blending into each other, charged with the mysterious emotional weight of past memories. It is, of course, in dreams that the image-making power of the psyche is freest and most operative; hence it seems fitting to compare the film with the dreaming mind rather than the mind operating consciously in the act of poetic creation.

The film appears to the spectator as a waking dream—it distorts, compresses, abolishes space and time as it builds a world of images around the hypnotized spectator; the huge shadows stir suppressed impulses as they assume the shape of the mythic prototypes of the unconscious life. The film images have greater psychic depth than those of a stage play because they do not dramatize or imitate reality but that world of fantasies which every man carries within himself.

The images of Cocteau's films defy the laws of nature. Props are always used suggestively with a hint that they themselves are part of the intimate life of the actors. To a far greater extent than in his plays he has been able to use *décor qui bouge* in his films. The camera always finds the unexpected angle from which the event is illuminated in a new and true perspective. The image does not merely pass across the screen; it unfolds, using the full space of the screen, living organically with its background and every other object represented, painted in the infinite range of colors from white to black. Cocteau encourages his actors to be larger than life, to be the phantasms of the unconscious that they become on the huge movie screen.

The film image, while related to the gag or *truc* of the early plays, benefits from the medium itself, from the catalytic power of the movie camera and screen. The parade which seems gaudy and unconvincing on the stage, touches the deepest unconscious realms of the mind where the mainsprings of sexual and religious feeling are hidden. In this realm of pure subjectivity, a realm beyond logic, nothing is allowed to retain its original shape or form; the unconscious mind transforms each image which reaches it into a version of itself. The logic of plot and character, as generally presented on the screen or in the theater, seems flat and trivial, irrelevant; Cocteau speaks in the language of the unconscious, a language beyond mere abstraction, the language of prophecy and madness.

The film *Orphée,* released in 1950, represents Cocteau's last major venture into the medium. It revives many of the themes of *Le Sang d'un poète,* shows us the poet as hero and dramatizes his flight from the world and his discovery of the meaning of art.

The action of the film begins in the Café des Poètes, where Orphée, the poet laureate, observes that an elegant woman, the Princess, is very interested in a young avant-garde poet, Cégeste. There is a fight, and, while attempting to get away, Cégeste is killed by two motorcyclists who roar up in front of the café. Orphée and the dead Cégeste are carried off by the Princess in her Rolls Royce; the car moves across a strange landscape; its radio emits enigmatic messages. Finally, accompanied now by the motorcyclists, they arrive at a dilapidated château; here the Princess revives Cégeste, who recognizes her as his own Death. They pass through a mirror, leaving Orphée behind. The chauffeur, Heurtebise, drives Orphée back to his home.

Orphée finds his wife Eurydice entertaining Aglaonice, director of the Club for Bacchantes. He is furious and forces Aglaonice to leave. Then, ignoring Eurydice, he spends hours trying to decipher the messages which continue to come from the car. Eurydice decides to go to her old friends, the bacchantes, to complain about Orphée; on the way, she is killed by the same motorcyclists.

Orphée begs Heurtebise to help him find his wife again, and so the chauffeur points out that the Princess has left her magic gloves in the bedroom, after a nocturnal visit. Orphée and Heurtebise pass through the mirror and find themselves in the château once again; but a trial is in progress. The Princess is accused of loving Orphée, Heurtebise of unconsciously loving

Eurydice. The court agrees to let Orphée retrieve his wife if he will never look at her.

This clause makes their life unbearable; finally, Eurydice forces Orphée to look at her and thus dies a second time. At the same moment, the bacchantes and the avant-garde enemies of Orphée appear in a mob, accusing Orphée of having killed Cégeste. He is shot and dies; but Heurtebise, aided by the motorcyclists, manages to carry off the poet's body in the Rolls Royce.

In the "zone intermédiaire" between life and death Orphée meets the Princess, who makes Orphée promise that he will never forget her; then, with the help of her assistants, she returns Orphée and Eurydice to life. The author comments: "A poet's Death must sacrifice herself to make him immortal." The film ends with the arrest of the Princess, who turns to receive her punishment, knowing that she has transgressed both divine and human law.

The 1950 *Orphée* differs radically from the play, produced in 1926, and is richer in spectacle and "poésie du théâtre" than this play or *Le Sang d'un poète*. Cocteau had all the resources of modern film technique at his disposal, and the images of *Orphée* are the most splendid that he has created. The scenes in the Café des Poètes, the ride across a mysterious countryside in the Rolls Royce, accompanied by masked motorcyclists, the passage through the "zone intermédiaire" which was filmed at night in the ruins of Saint-Cyr, Orphée's pursuit of his Death through a deserted city, the varied passages through mirrors, all these are striking visualizations of Cocteau's private dream which becomes our own.

Cocteau's discontinuous poetry finds its metaphor in the radio of the Rolls Royce, a gift to Orphée from the Princess. This radio speaks to Orphée in the language of a radical poetry, a poetry from beyond the grave, each image separate and intact, mysterious in its autonomy: "Jupiter gives wisdom to those he wishes to destroy." "The black crepe of little widows is a true feast of sunlight." "Silence goes more quickly backwards." "A single glass of water lights up the world." [6]

One of these lines, broadcast to Orphée, is from the pen of Guillaume Apollinaire: "The bird sings with its fingers." Apollinaire was the first poet to discover the poetic value of the machine, its countless human analogies and its affective role in modern culture. It was not merely that the mechanical marvels of the twentieth century were his metaphors; the free-ranging poetic sensibility—free yet turning continuously in the same patterns—seemed to him machine-like, just as Valéry and later Cocteau were to insist on the mechanical aspects of poetry, poetry as problem-solving. The radio of *Orphée* is perhaps the central metaphor of this whole historical process: A machine teaches the poet Orphée the secret of poetry; another machine, in the hands of Cocteau, who is himself a poet, records the lesson on film. The very substance of this lesson is a paean to the machine—a celebration of the device of spectacle, the visual pun, the sight gag, the linguistic equation. They are machines from which humanity is not absent.

Orpheus
and analogy

Orphée's speech is in the great prologue tradition: It commands us to enter the realm of illusion and warns us of the consequences if we fail through our indifference or distraction.

The single act is divided into thirteen scenes. In 1920, Cocteau tells us, the play was conceived in five acts. But each year it was shortened by an act, with the result, he says, that by the time of its completion in 1925 the comic and tragic aspects of the play were inextricably mixed. It was no longer possible to say whether the play was comedy or tragedy. Cocteau had gone beyond the conventional genres to create one of his own.

In scene 1, Orphée is trying to interpret a message which the horse is tapping out with his foot. Eurydice, who feels supplanted by this oracular beast, nags at Orphée. Then Orphée declares that through the horse he has discovered himself: "This horse enters my night and leaves it like a diver. He brings back phrases from it. Don't you see that the least of these phrases is more astonishing than all the poems in the world? I would give my complete works for a single one of these little phrases wherein I listen to myself as you listen to the ocean in a sea shell. Not serious? What do you require, my little one? I discover a world. I turn my skin inside out. I track the unknown."

This is the first statement of the change which will be operated in all the characters before the end of the play. It is symbolized by the final rising of the set into the sky. Orphée is in the process of discovering his true self through the horse, which may be interpreted variously as the devil, the unconscious, or perhaps simply as the marvelous. The horse has said previously to Orphée, "Madame Eurydice reviendra des enfers"—"Madame Eurydice will come back from hell." And Orphée has decided to enter this mysterious sentence in the annual Thracian poetry contest. Also in this scene, we are told of the danger which threatens Orphée and Eurydice, namely, Aglaonice and her bacchantes, Eurydice's friends before her marriage. The bacchantes are the female dictators of artistic taste, very much like the group of hysterical women who wanted to blind Cocteau and Picasso with hatpins after the opening of *Parade*.

Scenes 2 and 3 introduce Heurtebise, Cocteau's favorite angel. The name Heurtebise, Cocteau tells us, has a mysterious origin: "One day, as I was going to see Picasso, rue La Boétie, I felt, in the elevator, that I was growing side by side with something inexpressibly terrible which would be eternal. A voice cried to me, 'My name is on the plaque,' a shock woke me, and I read on the copper plaque of the handles: ELEVATOR HEURTE-BISE."[1] The name stuck with Cocteau, literally haunted him for months, although when the play had finally been completed and he looked again at the plaque, the name Heurtebise had been replaced by Otis-Pifre.

This is not the only strange event connected with the play. At the last rehearsal of the play, which was being held in Cocteau's apartment, at the words, "With these gloves you will pass through mirrors as if they were water," there was a loud, shattering noise, and the cast discovered that the bathroom mirror was pulverized. The first performance of *Orphée* in Mexico was interrupted by an earthquake. The theater was rebuilt, and the performance of the play started over, when, suddenly, it was interrupted again, this time definitively, by the death of the actor who played the role of Orphée, just before he was supposed to make his exit from the mirror.

Cocteau implies that Death was taking revenge on him for exposing so many of her secrets. One suspects that he feels, or would like to feel, that his play put him in league with mysterious supra-rational forces. Much of the impact of the play arises from the author's apparent feeling of complicity with things eschatological. This may be attributed to the influence of opium, for Cocteau was strongly addicted to the drug at this time.

Heurtebise is, by profession, a *vitrier,* or glazier. On his back he carries panes of glass of various sizes. When Heurtebise makes his entrance, then kneels, hands crossed on his breast, his glass sparkling in the lights, the virile golden angels of the Renaissance are instantly called to mind; it is the pose of the Annunciation. But there is further proof of his identity. While Heurtebise is repairing a window, the chair on which he is standing is pulled out from under him. He does not fall, and Eurydice, who sees him, is struck with fear and accuses him of being of the same race as the horse. Since he is a guardian angel, Heurtebise agrees to help Eurydice. Aglaonice is willing to exchange a powerful poison for a compromising letter which Eurydice has in her possession. With the poison, Eurydice will kill the horse. Along with the poison from Aglaonice, Heurtebise brings an envelope in which to put the letter that Eurydice is returning. Eurydice inserts the letter in the envelope and licks the glue. Shortly after, they realize that she herself has been poisoned by the treachery of Aglaonice.

In scene 6, while Heurtebise has gone to look for Orphée, Death and her two assistants, Azraël and Raphaël, emerge from the mirror. She wears an evening gown, the assistants are dressed as surgeons with masks and rubber gloves. Then begins the ritual which must be performed before Death can claim Eurydice. A vacuum cleaner whirs offstage—incantations, machines.

A rather effective device is employed at this point. One of the assistants asks a "plant" in the audience to lend him a watch, necessary for the termination of the ritual. The implication is that death is not remote. Common objects that surround us may be plotting our death, and we may frequently be Death's assistants, though perhaps without full awareness. Next there is a great deal of "business." Azraël counts like a referee counting a knock-out, Raphaël slowly executes naval code signals, Death follows a white thread to the room where Eurydice is lying and returns with a dove that flies away. They cut the thread, repack their suitcases and exit through the mirror. But in their haste, Death has forgotten her red rubber surgeon's gloves on the table.

In scene 7, Heurtebise returns with Orphée. It is too late. Eurydice is already dead. Orphée laments and vows that he will go to Hell to search for her. Heurtebise explains that in exchange for the gloves, Death may be willing to strike a bargain. Orphée puts on the gloves and penetrates the mirror. Cocteau chooses the mirror as the doorway to death because there appears to be a world behind the mirror, but it is a world which we cannot penetrate in our normal state. And he makes this clever amplification: "I shall tell you the secret of secrets. Mirrors are the doors by which Death comes and goes. Tell it to no one. Besides, watch yourself all your life in a mirror and you will see Death working like bees in a glass hive."

The passage into and return from Hell take place out of time. This is indicated by a brief eighth scene which is repeated, after the intermission: The postman knocks, speaks with Heurtebise, and finally slips a letter under the door. After a repetition of the identical action (scene 8bis) Orphée emerges from the mirror. This device prefigures the crumbling smokestack of *Le Sang d'un poète* and points to Cocteau's concern with objective or real time as opposed to subjective time.

In scene 9, Orphée and Eurydice attempt to resume their normal life, with the condition, of course, that Orphée does not look at his wife. At first, all is well, but after a short while, Orphée and Eurydice fall to quarreling as at the start of the play. Now everything is aggravated by the fact that they cannot face each other. Finally in a fit of temper, Orphée loses his balance and looks at Eurydice by accident. The lights darken, and Eurydice disappears.

At this point, Orphée opens the letter which the postman had delivered in scene 8. It warns him that his poem "Madame Eurydice Reviendra Des Enfers" has awakened the fury of the bacchantes. The initial letters, when taken together, form an insult for the contest judges—MERDE. Orphée cries: "The horse has tricked me!" As the drums of the bacchantes are heard, he announces that he will face them. He will not try to escape, as Heurtebise suggests. And Cocteau tells us: "The spell of the horse is ended. Orphée becomes transfigured."

Orphée goes joyously forth to face the bacchantes: "What does the marble, in which a sculptor carves a masterpiece, think? It thinks: He hits me, he spoils me, he insults me, he breaks me, I'm lost. This marble is stupid. Life is sculpting me, Heurtebise! It is making a masterpiece. I must accept its blows without understanding. I must stiffen myself. I must accept, hold still, help out, collaborate, let it finish its work." With these words, he rushes onto the balcony to be torn apart by the stones of the bacchantes.

In scene 10, in answer to the terrible complaints of the severed head, Eurydice comes into the room out of the mirror. The couple are reunited. Eurydice leads the now invisible body of Orphée into the mirror.

Scene 11. Frightened by the arrival of the police, Heurtebise picks up the severed head and places it on the pedestal. The commissioner enters and tells Heurtebise that public opinion has swung in favor of Orphée. The city prepares to receive his body in triumph. This is the ironic posthumous glory paid to so many poets. The commissioner begins to question Heurtebise. Meanwhile, Eurydice beckons from the mirror. The head of Orphée, on the pedestal, whispers to Heurtebise to follow her. In scene 12, the head replies to the questions which the commissioner thinks he is asking Heurtebise (the latter has already followed Eurydice into the mirror).

There is a triple confusion when the head of Orphée, which the commissioner thinks is really Heurtebise, replies that his name is Jean Cocteau and gives Cocteau's address. Again Cocteau tells us that this is make-believe and not reality. As at the beginning of the play, we have a plea and a threat. But this device is more than a mere reminder that Jean Cocteau is the author of the play. It is more than a warning not to make the mistake which was made by Orphée's unfriendly public. Somehow the author does not trust the play to maintain the dramatic illusion; so he purposely breaks into that illusion by giving his own name and address. By a curious double irony, this intervention only makes the illusion stronger. It mingles reality with the obvious fictions of the play and enhances that sense of complicity between the author and the mysterious forces of *outre-tombe* of which Cocteau has often spoken in connection with this play. In even the most realistic play esthetic distance is never lost. We know that we are in a theater and that what we are witnessing is only the *imitation* of an action. Cocteau suddenly crosses this esthetic distance and enters the play himself. Yes, the play is a fiction, he seems to say, but its truth is not a fiction. The device is a bold and effective one, indicative of Cocteau's intuitive grasp of the dramatic method.

Scene 13 shows the return of Orphée, Eurydice and their angel as the settings mount on wires into the loft. This is the fairy tale happy ending, achieved so effectively in the film *La Belle et la bête*. The same sense of things being at last in order is achieved in the exit of the blinded Œdipus, accompanied by his family, in *La Machine infernale*.

In this final scene it is as if Orphée and Eurydice were seeing their home for the first time. "They smile. They breathe a new calm." Orphée, who, we must not forget, is a priest, recites the following prayer: "God, we thank you for having assigned to us our house and home as our sole paradise and for having opened your paradise to us. We thank you for having sent us Heurtebise, and we accuse ourselves of not having recognized our guardian angel. We thank you for saving Eurydice because, for love, she killed the devil disguised as a horse and lost her own life in consequence. We thank you for having saved me because I adored poetry and because poetry is you. Amen."

The term *truc* is a pejorative term which Cocteau rehabilitates and makes his own with the apothegm: "Le truc c'est l'art." A *truc* is simply a device. It may be verbal, a play on words. Orphée opens with a near pun. The horse is tapping out a message with his foot and has gone as far as the letters M.E.R. Eurydice, who represents here and throughout the play the common sense view of the spectator, sarcastically tells Orphée not to insist on learning the rest of the message. But instead of tapping D.E., the horse adds C.I., MERCI, instead of MERDE. Now this is first of all a gag. It is a gag which plays on our expectation of something off-color and then turns it back on us. As a good *truc* should, it surprises us, first in our expectation and then in the reversal of our expectation. Like most of Cocteau's *trucs,* it comes very near to shocking us, to provoking, in a minor way, the "scandal" which Cocteau considers an important attribute of any work of art.

The verbal *truc* or pun which opens *Orphée* also possesses a kind of meaning for the play as a whole. Or we might say that it has overtones which add resonance to the play. *Merde* is the most common of all epithets of negation and may be read as a dadaistic insult to the public, a kind of gratuitous small-boy thumbing of the nose. Anything may happen, it seems to say, and I don't care if it does. Notice that Orphée is condemned by the bacchantes precisely because his poem is interpreted to read MERDE. This seems to imply that even without wanting to, a poet must insult his public. There is a degree of irony also in the way in which Cocteau proves to us that our subconscious is only too ready to play a slightly off-color game, a suggestion that perhaps we should cast off our prejudices and inhibitions and follow our subconscious into the play. Perhaps then we would not feel insulted. The effectiveness of the gag is increased by the fact that it is a dumb animal, a horse, which is the author's spokesman. The joke would be less effective in another context.

These explanations, however, are tentative and inconclusive. The pun is not altogether clear. It might even be taken to mean that the whole play is a joke or mystification. It is not firmly anchored in the context of the scene, and ultimately, it is the joke that dominates the whole episode. For one brief moment the play is suspended while the device is communicated to us. The same might be said of the scene in which Orphée's head gives the name of Jean Cocteau. Like the device of spectacle, the *truc* exists for itself rather than for the play as a whole.

Trucs of situation or character are even more common than verbal *trucs* in Cocteau's severely written play. Let us take, for instance, the character Death. She is a beautiful woman. This is a familiar allegorizing of the death theme. Allegory is such a highly artificial convention for the modern theater-goer that we should expect the allegorical device to be reflected elsewhere in the play in order to achieve esthetic coherence. The use of the horse is allegorical. Further, the mythical plot with its disregard for realism is highly allegorical. Allegory then seems to be one of the play's fundamental devices.

As we did with the pun, let us begin by seeing how much meaning we can extract from the personification of death. In the same way that death presents itself in the tranquil guise of sleep, the character Death appears in the guise of a beautiful woman. There is very little sense of horror, because she is not only death, she is mystery, the unknown which the poet and his wife must pierce before they can become their true Selves. The personage Death symbolizes the state of death. But this, in its turn, becomes symbolic of other aspects of the human quest.

These observations seem to indicate a circularity which is fundamental to the play on all levels. X equals X and non-X at the same time. Everything is its opposite. An event or a character contains its own negation. Death, in some indefinable way, is life. The use of allegory, of something concrete to represent an abstraction, thus contributes to the essential characteristic of Cocteau's method: a kind of brilliant analogizing.

I say a "kind of analogizing," because the relationships which Cocteau constantly affirms in his poetic universe do not strictly meet the test of analogy. However, they are not mere associations, that is, relationships which are entirely personal and subjective. Analogy, in contrast to association, always implies some kind of logical relationship, based on the essential structure of reality. Analogy clearly implies the nature of the relationship between two objects, their real likeness and real difference. Analogy is the basis for simile and metaphor. Although an analogy may first be suggested by a gratuitous association, it must afterwards justify itself within the context of the comparison. If the analogy is not apparent, it must be validated by some working-out of the comparison. If, for instance, the poet compares his mistress to a mirror, he must go on to say that he sees his fate reflected in her eyes. Underlying the comparison is the poet's dependence on his mistress, a real relationship. And further, there is the material resemblance of the eyes to the glass of a mirror and the reflecting properties of both. Cocteau says that the Italian Futurist, Marinetti, looks at the Victory of Samothrace and sees a locomotive. This is an example of association.

The analogy of death with the quest for truth or happiness is partially valid. Both are terms of the quest; both represent states which the person who quests has not yet achieved and which are mysterious to him. The sexual attraction of a beautiful woman is a conventional representation of the attraction of other more spiritual forms of beauty. But despite the partial validity of the analogy, death and happiness are not and never will be interchangeable. This is a fact which Cocteau keeps obscure and which he even goes so far as to deny by the play's happy ending. Maybe, he seems to say, death and happiness *are* the same thing.

There is a suggestive but unclear relationship between the three terms of the allegorized analogy woman-death-happiness. The personification of death, unlike the analogy of the mirror, tends to obscure the fundamental difference between the opposites death-happiness. Its tendency is to deny the distinctions between two types of experience and reduce them to a common denominator of poetic excitement. What finally emerges is this excitement, rather than any statement about life or death. So despite the many overtones of meaning which we have been able to obtain from it, the personification of death is ultimately a *truc,* or device.

From this fundamental ambiguity we can proceed to others —the horse for instance. No single interpretation is completely satisfactory; not even that given by Orphée himself, "the devil in the form of a horse." *Orphée* was finished in 1925 while Cocteau was still a Catholic and under the influence of Jacques Maritain. The play was originally intended to deal with the Christian theme of the Incarnation. This Christian framework perhaps accounts for the diabolical aspect of the horse. In other ways, though, the horse is not malevolent. It would seem that in general the function of the horse is to bring Orphée into contact with a new zone of his own being. Orpheus, it will be remembered, was able to charm beasts by his singing, so there is irony in having him, in his turn, charmed by a beast. Cocteau frequently uses the nonhuman world of animals, plants or machines to demonstrate human truths. The horse was diabolical because he destroyed the peace of the family. But if the horse caused the separation of Orphée and Eurydice, he helps them, in the end, attain to the other-world of poetry and mystery. Heurtebise, who is a guardian angel, is a Christian anachronism in this play about Greece. The horse is his pagan equivalent, that is, a kind of genie or personal daemon.

Even if we accept these ambiguities relative to the horse, we have still not answered another fundamental question: Why a horse? Why not some other animal? There are not many clues, and again we have a symbol which is somehow willfully abstract, cut off from its ordinary reference and hence its widest aura of suggestion. Is there a reference to Pegasus, the winged horse, symbol of the poetic imagination? Are the strength and size of the horse suggestive of masculine virility? Cocteau may be suggesting here the link between poetry and sexuality. The horse is all these things and none of them. He is a papier-mâché head projecting through a hole in the wall and, at the same time, the symbol of many obscure things within man and beyond him.

We must either accept the ambiguity of the horse or decide that Cocteau had not sufficiently clarified the role which he wished to give it. The first alternative is supported by other very intentional ambiguities. Is Heurtebise a man or an angel?

It is noteworthy that in the film, Cocteau tells us specifically, Heurtebise is not an angel. Yet the play tells us that he is, despite the surprising anachronism involved. His obvious tenderness for Eurydice is a distinctly human trait. Both Orphée and Eurydice die and are reborn. Orphée is angry with Eurydice and seems to have little respect for her intelligence. Yet he loves her enough to descend into Hell to save her. In the myth, we may remember, Orphée turns to see Eurydice out of love and anguish. Here, he does it out of sheer peevishness, in a moment of anger. There is a further ambiguity in Death herself. Is she friend or enemy? In the film, she is on Orphée's side, actually falls in love with him and tries to help him in his combat with the infernal gods. In the play, she is an impartial functionary doing her duty. In all these examples we see a curious washing-out of contrasts, a reduction of everything to a common denominator of poetic excitement which is generated by the devices and seems intended to replace the tensions of a drama grounded in reality.

Many of Cocteau's devices are validated either by logic or by a spurious logic. He does not by any means operate in a purely poetic realm, but on the fringe, between two worlds as it were. There is a reservoir of meaning in the myth itself with its venerable relationships to literature and history. Cocteau profits by this, even though all the resonances of the myth are not picked up in the play. The language is sober and seems to disavow the determined "poetry" of the action. It is used skillfully to rationalize the improbable or the arbitrary aspects of the action. An example is the simile of the mirror in which,

Heurtebise says, we see Death at work in us like bees in a glass hive. Cocteau has quite arbitrarily chosen the mirror as the doorway to the land of the dead. This ingenious simile adds a momentary luster of truth to the assertion, at least sufficient truth to maintain the play's credibility. It cannot, of course, make the assertion any less arbitrary. No one really leaves the theater believing that Death is a woman who comes through the mirror. Yet the simile is valid in itself, and rationalizes us ahead into the land of the dead by a swift bit of pseudo or spurious logic.

Another form of coherence is achieved through the rather one-dimensional characterizations of Orphée and Eurydice. They argue and nag each other like any young couple in boulevard comedy. They are, in many respects, uncomplicated and eminently recognizable. They seem to be transplanted from some boulevard comedy into the world of myth with no visible strain. Along with the rubber gloves, the watch and other everyday objects, situations or expressions, they identify the world of the play for us. Their function is to reassure us that none of this is really unfamiliar. The main characters are those we see in the theater whenever a new play of Sacha Guitry or Henri Bernstein opens. The props might have come from the drugstore, our living room or our kitchen.

And thus we are led to the most important communication which the play makes. The play is not so highly symbolistic that it denies reality with its close-knit structures of human and essential relationships. But it does somehow drain reality of much of its significance through a resolute indifference to conventional meanings and implications. Anything real in it becomes the pretext for a lyrical excursion. And the play seems to tell us, in effect, that nothing real, not even death, need be considered as limiting the poetic power to transform. By a kind of willful autointoxication with images, we can remake the world as we choose. And, in fact, we must do so. Already in *Orphée* there is apparent a fear of the real world and a determination to ignore it or to escape from it; language is used as a means of evasion.

From this analysis of Cocteau's esthetics it seems apparent that the poem is a vehicle which operates by analogy or by disguised association. This vehicle gives the appearance of logic and coherence in the face of reality and the verifiable emotional and spiritual experiences of mankind. Whenever it cannot give this appearance, it operates by spurious logic masked by verbal and spectacular brilliance. The *truc* or device is often employed instead of the self-justifying metaphor. The devices of spectacle in the early plays and the films, the emphasis on mechanical repetition as a substitute for logic, skirt true metaphor and fall under the rubric of association, an affective linking up of terms in the absence of rational content. The same procedure may be found in all of Cocteau's works; it is especially apparent in his lyric poetry.

This indifference to logic leads us to the final truth about Cocteau's esthetic. It derives from the tradition of Mallarmé, of art for art and pure poetry. In the last analysis, the forms of discourse which it considers as primarily valid are the fabrications of the imagination operating under psychological pressures, even without the verifications of the factual world. Poetry is a closed and hermetic system which we must enter by magic, in a state of trance, under the spell of Orpheus, rather than by the key of rational inquiry and analysis. We submit to a mystery, the mystery of style; behind this style lie psychological pressures which represent the second phase of Cocteau's mystery.

Cocteau
the hunted

"We are either the judge or the accused."
                    Journal d'un inconnu

"Jeanne d'Arc is my great writer. . . . Antigone is my other saint."
                    La Difficulté d'être

COCTEAU'S AFFECTION FOR JEAN-JACQUES ROUSSEAU IS NOT FOR-
tuitous. On the second page of his study of Rousseau he writes:
"I will not try to keep anyone from believing that Jean-Jacques
Rousseau was a sick man afflicted with a persecution complex.
But knowing as I do the patient method with which poets are
persecuted, I consider that my duty is to put my experience to
good use and demonstrate that if Rousseau was skinned alive,
he had his excuses, and that he was persecuted." [1] Cocteau's
friendship for Jean Genet is certainly due, in part, to an iden-

tification with the criminal-poet, whom Cocteau sees as another great symbol of social ostracism.

In the case of Cocteau, as in the case of Rousseau, it is difficult to say what constitutes persecution. Cocteau resents bitterly the attacks made on his person by the Surrealists or by such old friends as François Mauriac. The book by Mauriac's son, Claude, written while Claude Mauriac was a member of Cocteau's circle and a visitor at his home, is biased, unfair and malicious. Cocteau was justified in looking on it as a kind of treachery.[2] During the Occupation of France by the Germans, Cocteau's plays were forbidden by Vichy and severely criticized in the press. He was attacked and beaten up on the avenue des Champs-Elysées for refusing to salute the flag of the *Ligue des Volontaires Français contre le bolchevisme*. Even though he has often been treated unfairly by his friends, critics and the public at large, Cocteau's response to this situation has been somewhat abnormal. The idea of persecution has become part of his philosophy and the feeling of persecution his instinctive response to the world.

Examples of this feeling of persecution are especially numerous in *Journal d'un inconnu,* published in 1953 when Cocteau was sixty-three years old: "I am, no doubt, the most unknown and the most celebrated of poets." "What were my faults in the orchestra of blame which shatters my ears?" "If I write, I vex. If I make a film, I vex. If I paint, I vex. If I exhibit my painting, I vex; and I vex if I don't exhibit it. I have the gift of vexation." "Knowing my colleagues and my countrymen, I warn young people of the danger of 'what-will-people-say' that they run by associating with me."[3] Cocteau devotes an entire chapter, "D'une justification de l'injustice," to pardoning Maurice Sachs, Claude Mauriac, Gide, and others, for their attacks on him.

The most conclusive proof of this deep feeling of ostracism or social exile is to be found in the plays themselves and beginning as far back as the translation of *Antigone*.

Greece, the myth of Greece, has continually fascinated Cocteau. Like all myths, it represents many things; incest, for instance, and unnatural love, or style or implacable destiny. But the most fundamental and permanent reading of the myth is purity.

Greek art, Greek philosophy, the geometrical lines of the ancient temples, the moral and esthetic contours of the tragic heroes, symbolize for Cocteau the highest perfection of human nature. That perfection, which is the attainment of purity, is reached by a moral process which might be called an "emptying" of the self. The poet finds within himself a moral law, his own law, and he must strive to cancel every act that contradicts this morality. We are pure when we are ourselves. The criminal or the homosexual, in order to be pure, must contradict the morality which society attempts to impose on him. Pasiphaë, Œdipus and Alcibiades, true to their own abnormal instincts, are exemplars of this purity. Purity, in other words, is what we are and what the world would prevent us from being. We can attain it only by discovering our own deep uniqueness. Purity makes us mysterious, insofar as it sets us apart from each other.

It seems clear that Cocteau chose to translate *Antigone* because of a feeling of sympathy with its heroine. That sympathy is not very different from that which he has expressed for Jeanne d'Arc, Rousseau or Genet. All these personages have in common a persecution situation. In the majority of Cocteau's plays, there is some sort of persecution situation. *Antigone* is typical. And it is further typical that the heroine is persecuted for representing that very purity which distinguishes the sublime race of poets from other men and women.

Cocteau's shortened version of *Antigone* was given for the first time at the Atelier in Paris in 1922, with settings by Picasso, music by Honegger, costumes by Gabrielle Chanel, and Charles Dullin and Antonin Artaud in the roles of Créon and Tirésias. Cocteau spoke the part of the chorus, and Genica Atanasiou played Antigone.

Cocteau's brief, conscise prose style is not an unsuitable substitute for the Greek of Sophocles. Racine, like a tutelary god, seems to bless the undertaking. Greeks have spoken French before, and Cocteau has profited by, rather than succumbed to, the Racinian tradition. There is the dramatic unity of Racine in a different psychological and verbal context.

The rhythm of Cocteau's prose is nervous and abrupt. This quality and the extreme compression of the action combine to modernize *Antigone*. The accumulation of poetic detail, the reflection of the chorus (which Cocteau reduces to one voice) on the action, the heights and depths which we find in Sophocles, have been cut. "So reduced, concentrated, scoured, the work rolls on towards its climax like an express train." [4] The play is closer to the modern genre of melodrama than to

Greek tragedy. In shortening the speeches, Cocteau has lessened the stature of the characters, restricted their dimensions, making them more schematic and hence less able to awake the profound sympathy of the audience.

One has the impression, in reading the notes and stage directions, that *Antigone,* like *Roméo et Juliette,* was a *prétexte à mise en scène.* And it could scarcely have been otherwise, considering Cocteau's collaborators. But here, as in *Les Mariés,* Cocteau's theatricality serves a purpose fundamental to his conception of the theater. For example, the costumes "were put on over black tights. The ensemble evoking a carnival, sordid but royal, a family of insects." Or this expressionistic stage direction: "Antigone and Créon speak face to face; their foreheads touch." Again, just before the arrival of the messenger who announces to the queen Eurydice the death of Hémon, her son, there is a musical interlude during which a masked statue walks across the stage.

Details such as this serve to remind us that we are not Greeks and this is not Sophocles. We are seeing a myth of Greece interpreted at a remove of twenty-four hundred years. Perhaps Cocteau is also saying that the very meaning of the myth is inherent in its theatricality. Antigone, like all of Cocteau's heroes or heroines, is a poet, and her heroism consists in a kind of bravado which is not chiefly significant as an act of religious faith or of family loyalty or even as defiance of a tyrant. In defying Créon and burying her brother, Polynice, she is not the figure of resistance to oppression that she becomes in Anouilh's version of the play; the stylization of the play portrays her deed as gesture, as the expression of the theatrical in life—an action unexpected, audacious, gratuitous, having little validity beyond itself. There is a strong and generic relationship between *Antigone* and Cocteau's first original drama, *Orphée.*

Orphée, which is concerned with a poet's triumph over life and death, implied, by its very style and structure, some kind of statement about the importance of pure poetry or what we might call imaginative autoexcitement. Poetry, taken in a broad and undefined sense, is the chief value in life. Such a value has an imperative character. The obligation to produce poetry is, for Cocteau, a "moral law." But to obey one's moral law, as Cocteau sees it, is always dangerous. In *Orphée* we see the persecution situation in its fundamental form. The poet understands that he is governed by a moral law which he must obey at all cost, even at the risk of losing his life. For Orphée, that moral law entails a martyrdom inflicted by his public.

Cocteau's attacks on the Parisian public are ample retaliation for whatever persecution he has suffered at its hands. His conception of the outcast poet, in advance of his age, a living indictment of conservatism and prejudice, is an implicit criticism of the public. Beginning as far back as *Le Coq et l'Arlequin* (1918), his distrust and resentment of the public is already wholly articulated: "Whatever the public reproaches you for, cultivate it. It is you." "Indolence of the public. Armchair and belly of the public. The public is ready to adopt no matter what new game provided that nothing is changed, once it knows the rules. Its hatred of the creator is a hatred of someone who changes the rules of the game." " 'Why do you do it that way?'

the public asks. 'Because you wouldn't,' replies the creator." [5]

Such acid judgments are to be found in many other works. In *Le Journal d'un inconnu*, Cocteau attacks the *public d'élite* which composes the opening-night audience. He says that he much prefers the naïve movie audience which is capable of being moved and of catching the spirit of a work. Cocteau may be attacking in self-defense. By and large, he has not fascinated or moved his audiences as much as he has amused them. As he sees it, however, it is the poet's moral law and the presence of that law in his work which disconcert the audience: "That morality which takes form will become an insult." [6]

Orphée's moral law, contrary to Antigone's, is entirely without content. He is not defending any principle except, perhaps, his right to be different. But as does Antigone, Orphée achieves the purity of self-sacrifice. He is decapitated by the screaming women, who throw his head back into the room. Poets have not always been outcasts and exiles, but, since the Romantic period, to a great degree, the role of the poet has been nonconformism. The affirmation of the right to be different is Cocteau's central theme. It is on this principle that his heroes engage the world, and from it flows his vision of tragedy.

The play narrates a triumph over death and the attainment of wisdom through death. Death is not only the death of the body. It is a symbol of the night which surrounds us and which, even in life, we must try to pierce. The theme of triumph over the public intersects the theme of triumph over death. The fact that he alone penetrates this mystery sets the poet apart. His knowledge is an insult; his conduct is a denial of social behavior.

The poet's martyrdom is the seal of his frame. When finally he is torn to bits, we know that he has achieved greatness.

There are other plays in which the purity-persecution theme has an important part. Œdipe in *La Machine infernale* is a mortal persecuted by the gods. In most of the plays, however, the poet is a victim of society. It is in his most recent play, *Bacchus,* produced by Jean-Louis Barrault at the Théâtre Marigny on December 20, 1951, that Cocteau has made his final formulation of this theme, as if to prove its conclusive importance.

Like so many other of his plays, *Bacchus* produced a "scandal." Cocteau considers scandal a recognition of true originality —"beauty, its rapidity, its adroitness, its fire provoke the same scandal. . . ." [7] But the form which scandal took on the night of December 20th was especially displeasing to Cocteau. Immediately after the last curtain, and just as the audience began to applaud, François Mauriac rose dramatically and left the theater in a gesture of protest. On December 29th, he addressed a letter to Cocteau in the pages of the *Figaro littéraire.* He said that *Bacchus* was sacrilegious, that Cocteau had bound his venerable Mother, the Church, to a pillar of the Marigny and whipped her. Several days later Cocteau replied in *France-Soir* that Mauriac was not able to stand a friend's success, that he was a hypocrite who criticized in other people the scabrous goings-on in which he took such obvious delight in his own novels. Cocteau concluded with a dramatic "Adieu" and the statement that he would never again address another remark to Mauriac.

The invited opening-night audience had been loud in its applause. But the play was hissed by the gallery composed of students and artists, the audience that Cocteau really wanted to please. Cocteau claims that the play was a triumph and that it closed after a limited number of performances only because Barrault had other engagements.

Bacchus is written in Cocteau's latest style, a concise realism that was well adapted to *Les Parents terribles* but has less relevance here. It is a hodge-podge of all Cocteau's theories, an anthology of remarks by Radiguet, Picasso and Genet. Too often, it is Cocteau imitating himself.

The setting is sixteenth century Germany. At the start of the play, we learn from Lothar and Christine, brother and sister, that a curious ceremony is about to be held in the city. It is the Bacchus festival during which, every five years, a young man from the village is crowned king and reigns for seven days with absolute power. Lothar wants to enter the contest, but Christine restrains him, reminding him that their brother, Ulrich, died as a result of an earlier festival. Lothar and Christine admit to each other that they have been attending secret meetings of the Lutheran sect. On one occasion, Lothar has seen their father, the Duke, at such a meeting. Conclusion: He must be a Protestant leader. Next, we are shown a meeting of the leaders of the town, the Duke, the Bishop, the Provost and a visiting legate from Rome, Cardinal Zampi. The Cardinal is very mysterious and menacing, acts as if he holds great power, but never uses it. He has come to investigate the state of unrest in the district; however, he never makes any concrete discoveries or comes to grips with the Protestants. The whole Protestant intrigue is superfluous; we might contrast Sartre's *Le Diable et le bon Dieu,* written simultaneously with *Bacchus* and also set in sixteenth century Germany. In Sartre's play, the Protestant rebellion and the revolt of the peasants function effectively in the plot.

The meeting is being held to discuss the festival. The Duke says that his daughter Christine has suggested a plan which will allow them to control the festival from behind the scenes. She wishes to crown the village idiot, a young man named Hans, who will, presumably, do whatever she commands him. In the final scenes of Act I, the Cardinal and the others interview Hans to see if the plan is workable. It is during this interview in Act I, scene 7, that Hans is asked to repeat the Lord's Prayer. It was the Amen as much as anything that offended Mauriac:

L'ÉVÊQUE

Ne nous laissez pas succomber à la tentation et délivrez-nous du mal. Ainsi soit-il.

HANS

Si soit-il. . .

The high point of this first act is the interrogation of Hans and the unexpected conduct of the young madman. Even the shrewd Cardinal is convinced that the madness of Hans is authentic. The act ends with the decision to crown Hans and a listing of privileges that he will enjoy—a guard of honor, whatever dwelling in the town he chooses and the right to enter the church on horseback.

Hans is the central character. Although he is a peasant and a madman, his beauty gives him a kind of nobility. His madness has a strange origin. A group of young noblemen met him while they were on a hunt, set their dogs on him and chased him like an animal, until he went mad. This man-hunt, like the imprisonment of Antigone or the stoning of Orphée, symbolizes the persecution situation. It is beautifully described in Hans's own words in Act III, scene 8: "The pack moved, splattered, cried, barked. I was sweating like a beast. I became a beast. It had something so mad about it that fear became madness and was no longer fear, but a monstrous music of savage horns, of laughter, of beating heart, whistling ears, of horses and of water turned to foam. There were plants that tried to tangle my legs and leaves which stuck to my eyes. I caught myself on roots. Hate was sounding its horn."

This nightmare flight brings to the surface a sense of fear implicit in all Cocteau's heroes, a secret prescience that the world is going to turn on them and destroy them. It is true, Hans is hunted because he is a peasant, and the play might be considered to be making a commentary on social conditions in sixteenth century Germany; however, the social criticism is only incidental here (as it is not in *Le Diable et le bon Dieu*). When Hans achieves power, he does not make any systematic social reforms. His goal is anarchy. In Sartre's play, the hero, Goetz, achieves human solidarity by joining the proletarian revolution. Goetz is a man without allegiances, like Hans; but in the course of the play Goetz learns that allegiance is not arbitrary and that what we are will be determined finally by what we choose. From a condition of total freedom he moves toward involvement. Hans seeks only to affirm his freedom, and it is this very freedom that turns the world against him. The whole play represents the pursuit and hunting down of Hans until he dies, shot by Lothar, in the final scene. Hans is not a social reformer. He is a poet, in other words, the incarnation of what the world hates.

This play, written in the heyday of Sartre, shows how Cocteau was trying to renew himself while, at the same time, remaining faithful to his own credo. There is an odd unreality about it; for in the 1950's the joyous irresponsibility of the 1920's seems frivolous. There is no remounting the stream of history, and it is doubtful whether a viewpoint evolved under the stress of a particular set of circumstances can be brought up to date. There is something wistful about Cocteau's attempt at modernization; the force and significance of his work cannot be separated from the historical context which they helped to fashion.

In the first scene of Act II, Lothar tells the Duke and the Provost of a serious incident which took place shortly after the coronation of Hans. A group of young noblemen was jeering at the newly crowned Bacchus. After a scuffle, Hans threw one of them into the lake, where he drowned. Then in a terrible voice he exclaimed: "Let that be a lesson to you!" It now becomes clear that Hans is not an idiot and that he has tricked everyone in allowing himself to be crowned Bacchus. Hans had indeed lost his reason, but he regained it shortly after, when he was forced to watch a group of his friends being tortured by these same noblemen. He resolved to continue to feign madness in order to protect himself.

Most of the action, like the incident related above, takes place offstage and is presented by narration. Onstage we have only a series of pretentious discussions centering around a fairy tale which it is impossible to take seriously (precisely because it is not presented as a fairy tale). The fundamental weakness of *Bacchus* is a failure of plot. Hans is not persecuted for anything he *does,* and how else can attitude be defined except in action? Hans has no dramatic contact with any of the other characters of the play. He is the solitary *poète maudit,* the poet masquerading as madman and god, cut off from the rest of mankind. Hans cries out to the Cardinal (Act III, scene 7): "In my eyes this masquerade is not a masquerade." He demands to be taken seriously without, however, involving himself with the world and those around him in any relevant way. There is something pathetic and moving in these words. Cocteau has used them very often, pleading with his audiences again and again to take his masquerades seriously.

Although he does not have a program, Hans does not fail to take advantage of his powers. He opens the prisons, he preaches goodness (*la bonté*) to the crowd, he rides into church on horseback, he chases the merchants from the church steps. In Act II, scene 4, the Cardinal and Hans have their first important discussion.

The Cardinal demands to know Hans's intentions. Why is he stirring up trouble? preaching to the peasants? aiding the forces of revolt? Which side is he on? Hans answers simply: "I seek to remain pure." In other words, Hans belongs to no party; he takes no sides. He searches his truth in himself rather than in a cause. His only aim is to "Stir the forces of love which sleep. Abolish fear. Be good as most people are bad. Love as they hate. Kill hatred. Not to know where that will lead me." (Act II, scene 6) He affirms his liberty with these words: "If I belonged to a party, I should betray my free soul with that party or the party with my free soul. Besides, my teacher put me on guard against that moral comfort which flatters our sloth. To engage oneself in a party is a comfort, since that party supports us and spares us the anguish of nuances to the advantage of a single color." (Act II, scene 6)

In this same scene Hans finally convinces the Cardinal that he is completely "free," and the Cardinal exclaims:

Per Baccho, little brother. Are you a real innocent?

HANS

If you mean by that the contrary of a culprit, I admit it. I admit that I am an innocent. Is it a crime?

THE CARDINAL

I should have preferred to see you plead guilty. I would at least know before whom I stand.

HANS

If I understand you, you prefer a culprit to someone innocent.

THE CARDINAL (*thoughtfully*)

Perhaps. Innocence is sometimes dangerous. The culprit is discovered. The innocent escapes us. Potentially guilty. If the criminal
expresses himself, he is judged on his act. If the innocent acts, he
causes only anarchy.

We see where all this is leading: to the bonfire and the stake.
But here, as in *La Machine infernale,* failure is really a triumph.

HANS

No doubt you are right to burn us alive, Monseigneur. Everything
is consumed, and fire is a beast which consumes itself. I don't claim
that one may interrupt such a holocaust, if it is life, but one may
perhaps give it the atmosphere of an evening fête, a fire of joy. I
will be an embarrassing and unbearable martyr. For I would like
a dance around my pyre, not to glorify my defeat, but my victory.

THE CARDINAL

What victory?

HANS

Failure. There is no true victory without failure. The victors are
left to die of their victory, and the beaten become victors because
everyone cares for them and takes them in charge. Christ knew it.

As Cocteau tells us in *Opium,* "Whoever does not understand
failure is lost." [8] And Hans exclaims in Act III, scene 5, "If they
burn me, I win. If I escape, I lose." So the circle closes. The
hero, in search of purity, is crucified by the world because of

that very purity; but this crucifixion is essential to the attainment of his goal.

The play reaches for meaning on a mythical level, and once again Cocteau has made use of legend. Anthropologists have told us about the many types of rituals in which a god or godman is sacrificed. All tragedy draws its validity from this mythical substratum, which is based, in its turn, on the need of the community for heroes who can surpass the limits of the human condition.

Cocteau may very well tell us that he is dramatizing a Byzantine legend which is five thousand years old, but he has not brought the myth into modern perspective as he did in *Orphée*. Hans is less of a hanged or drowned god than he is a young man who is not quite sure which way to turn. In *Journal d'un inconnu,* Cocteau characterizes the play thus: "I tackled the theme of the disorder of youth amidst the dogmas, the sects, the obstacles thrust in its path. In prey to offers of help . . . it seeks to remain free. Its disordered liberty glides between the obstacles until finally it cracks up." [9] But what relevance does this have to the other themes of the play? Like the myth of the hanged or drowned god, this theme is not clearly realized. The real myth which Hans dramatizes—that of the solitary, melodramatic, prophetic *poète maudit*—is not what the play is supposed to be about. Where plot is deficient, neither intention nor realization can be clarified. The play is written on two levels which do not cohere or function together.

Act III takes place on the last day of the festival. The Duke, the Cardinal, and the rest, are gathered to discuss a means for saving Hans from the fury of the crowd. He has made one "mistake" after another. The taxes which he abolished will be doubled; he has offended the nobles by ordering his troops to disperse the funeral procession of the young man he had drowned. The whole town has turned against him. But the Cardinal has found a solution. Hans will sign an abjuration, admitting that he has been in the service of the Protestants, and the Cardinal will then conceal him in a monastery where he will take holy orders. Christine and Hans have been in love since the end of Act II. The Cardinal calls on her to persuade Hans to save himself. But just as Orphée went to meet the bacchantes, Hans rushes to the window to harangue the crowd once again. There, he is pierced by an arrow. Lothar has shot him, out of fear that Hans, who has become his hero and ideal, may not remain pure.

The poet is misunderstood even by those who love him; he is the victim of a conspiracy against which his purity, his intense need to be himself, makes him helpless. He refuses the weapons of deceit, conformity and compromise; rallying all the metaphors of steadfastness and solitary resistance to outside pressure, reciting his litany of saints—Antigone, Jesus Christ, Jeanne d'Arc, Rousseau and the rest—he lets himself be torn to pieces, dismembered, made a human sacrifice. He is simultaneously stubborn child, rebellious adolescent, revolutionary and saint; it is not always easy to distinguish his motives since, in the last analysis, what predominates is the desire to have his own way.

Cocteau's heroes are portrayed in the same fashion that he portrays himself, as pursued, punished, exiled or threatened.

He himself is largely the author of the legend which portrays him as a hunted man, even if he did not intentionally bring about all the events on which this legend is based. There is something about which Cocteau feels guilty, something about his life or his personality which deserves punishment.

We arrive here at a theme which is completely suppressed in Cocteau's work. Since there is no official biography of Cocteau, it seems fitting to end this phase of our inquiry here, with a final observation. The homosexual frequently sees himself as one who is beyond the pale of society. What may seem to other people, who observe him, only an unfortunate accident of his psychic life, becomes, in his eyes, cause and symbol of a permanent ostracism from society.

Whatever its ultimate psychic origin, it seems clear that Cocteau envisages his own situation (and it is himself he is symbolizing in the youthful heroes and heroines of his plays) as one of passive suffering. The defeat and failure of his heroes do not have the cosmic overtones of the fall of Sophocles' Œdipus or Shakespeare's Macbeth. They are rather like children who choose to be disobedient in order that they may be punished, inflicting thereby a certain remorse on their parents. These characters desire and seek out punishment as a means of allaying their guilt at being different. This represents a transcendence, an involvement with others. They engage the world as victims to be punished, thereby transferring a part of their own guilt to those who punish them. To borrow an image from Cocteau's *Bacchus,* these characters force the rest of us to come and dance around the bonfire on which they are being sacri-

ficed. The element of exaggeration here is obvious. Cocteau has
not been burned at the stake; in fact, he has recently become
a member of the French Academy. But he kills off his characters just the same. They are expiatory victims in a universe to
which, deep down, Cocteau has never become reconciled.

Cocteau never dramatizes the suppressed theme of homosexuality. Instead, he extends the metaphor of persecution to
cosmic dimensions. In *La Machine infernale* the gods themselves become the persecutors. Cocteau invariably refuses to find
the truth of his characters' tragedy within themselves, where it
belongs. Instead, he blames it on obscure forces beyond men,
on their destiny. Through *Bacchus* we are brought to another
mystery: What is the nature of this destiny which drives such
lighthearted heroes to their doom?

Liberty and the infernal machine

La Machine infernale, FIRST PRODUCED BY LOUIS JOUVET IN
1934, might be considered the most extraordinary of all
Cocteau's improvisations. It is as if he had been challenged to
take the myth of Œdipus and ring as many changes on it as
possible, exploiting every irony and *double-entendre*. The high
point of the play, Act III, the wedding night of Œdipe and
Jocaste, is developed with the versatility of a Molière comedy.
But again, as in *Orphée,* the predominant tone is neither comic
nor tragic. It is something else, some special genre of Cocteau's

own creation, with a continuity of feeling and expression which is not easily accounted for.

The settings were created by Christian Bérard. They enclose a small platform in the center of the stage where the action takes place. This is not the panoramic sweep of the open-air theater where the plays of Sophocles were performed. It is a reduction, and the whole mythic action of the play really passes outside the "nocturnal curtains" which surround the platform.

The play begins with an oracular prologue; Cocteau's resonant, prophetic voice has been heard in this role in' both the 1934 and 1954 productions. The Voice rehearses the story of the myth and enjoins the audience to look for the real story behind the entertainment they are about to witness. The play then begins, on the ramparts of Thebes, with a scene reminiscent of the opening of *Hamlet*.

Two soldiers are standing guard. Through them we learn that a plague is devastating the city and that to this disaster has been added another, the Sphinx. They discuss the identity of the Sphinx: Is it part woman? Is it a vampire? The younger soldier, fed up with guard duty, cries that he will go to challenge the Sphinx. Maybe there is only a riddle to be answered. And if there is, why shouldn't he be the one to do it? They further discuss a ghost which has appeared to them on successive nights: the ghost of Laius, their dead king. The captain-of-the-guard appears, and they repeat the story of the ghost to him. The ghost has asked the soldiers to call Jocaste and Tirésias, the high priest, as quickly as possible. He cannot appear directly to them because he can manifest himself only on the ramparts, near the sewers with their ectoplasmic vapors.

A short while later, Jocaste and Tirésias appear. The tone of this first act is predominantly comic. Jocaste has "that international accent of royalties"; she is vain, capricious, warmhearted. Tirésias, whom she calls "Zizi," forces himself to be patient with the queen. He helps her climb the stairs backwards so she will not have to look at her feet. When finally she meets and questions the young soldier who has seen the ghost, Jocaste is quite enchanted by his leg muscles and invites him to come and see her in the palace. She thinks wistfully that he is the same age as her long-lost son. This is a prelude to the sexual attraction between Œdipe and Jocaste when they are finally united in Act III.

They wait for the ghost, which does not appear. When at last he speaks, still invisible, none of them can hear him. Finally, when Jocaste and Tirésias have left the ramparts, Laius appears again to the soldiers. As one of the soldiers says: "When the carpenter arrives, the chair stops wobbling; when you enter the shoemaker's shop, your sandal stops rubbing; when you get to the doctor's, you no longer feel the pain. Go look for them! As soon as they get here, the ghost will disappear." The soldiers, with their rough, boyish innocence, can see the ghost. But the priests, the kings and queens, the generals, are blind to the truth, which is seen only by the simple and the pure in heart. Nothing can stop the destiny which must destroy Œdipe and Jocaste.

Act II begins with the announcement by the Voice that we are to witness the very thing of which Laius was trying to warn Jocaste: Œdipe, their son, approaches Thebes. On a hill which dominates the city, bathed in an eerie green light, Œdipe meets the Sphinx.[1] The Sphinx, like Death in *Orphée,* is a beautiful woman—"Death must be the most elegant woman in the world because she cares about nothing but herself." [2] Anubis, her servant, is a giant with long claws and the head of a jackal. Unlike the Death of *Orphée,* the Sphinx, who is really the goddess Nemesis, rebels against her task.

Cocteau seems to be anticipating a possible criticism of the Sphinx, on the grounds that a creature of pure fantasy is too arbitrary, when he causes her to say: "Why always act without purpose, without end, without understanding? So, for example, Anubis, why your dog's head? Why the god of the dead in the form that credulous men imagine him? Why in Greece an Egyptian god? Why a god with a dog's head?" Even the servants of the gods rebel at the arbitrariness of divine decree; however, it is not the gods of Olympus but Cocteau himself who is the creator of Anubis.

There are brief moments when the spell breaks down and the drama dissolves into fantasy. An example is the repartee of Œdipe and the Sphinx when they first meet. With this exception, the encounter with the Sphinx moves very rapidly by a series of charms, spells and transformations. His eyes shut, Œdipe counts to fifty. When he opens them, the young woman has mounted on the pedestal. She has become the Sphinx. Œdipe falls under her spell. Struggle as he will, he cannot move. The Sphinx pronounces a long magic charm which is necessary in order to accomplish her task. She winds him in her words like a net or silken thread:

Useless to close your eyes, to turn your head; for it is neither by song nor by my glance that I act. But more adroit than a blindman, more rapid than the gladiator's net, more subtle than lightning, more obstinate than a coachman, heavier than a cow, wiser than a student scratching his head over a column of figures, more rigged, fuller-sheeted, more anchored, more rocked than a ship, more incorruptible than a judge, more voracious than the insects, more blood-thirsty than the birds, more nocturnal than an egg, more ingenious than the Asiatic executioners, trickier than the heart, more un-self-conscious than the hand that tricks, more fatal than the stars, more attentive than the snake which moistens its prey with saliva; I secrete, I draw from myself, I release, I unwind, I unroll, I enroll so that it will suffice for me to wish these knots in order to make them and to think in order to tighten or un-tighten them; so narrow that it escapes you, so supple that you will imagine yourself victim of some poison, so hard that a blunder on my part would dismember you, so taut that a bow would draw forth between us a celestial plaint; buckled like the sea, the col-umn, the rose, muscled like the octopus, machined like the décors of a dream, above all invisible, invisible and majestic like the blood circulation of statues, a wire which binds you with the volubility of crazy arabesques of honey which fall on honey.

When Œdipe has finally succumbed to her spell, she asks him the riddle: "What animal walks on four feet in the morning, on two feet at noon, on three feet in the evening?" Even though he fails to answer, she does not allow Anubis to kill the helpless Œdipe. The Sphinx has fallen in love with this handsome young mortal. In the presence of Anubis, she asks the riddle again, and Œdipe triumphantly cries out the answer which she has already told him: "Man, of course, who crawls on four feet when he is a child, who walks on two feet when he is grown and who, when he is old, aids himself with the third foot of a cane." Man and his changing nature are the riddle of the Sphinx.

The Sphinx collapses, and Œdipe leaps free, crying "the victor!" and runs off in the direction of Thebes while the Sphinx laments. How could Œdipe not have seen that she spared him out of love? To pacify her wrath, Anubis tells her of the dreadful fate awaiting Œdipe. When Œdipe returns a moment later for a trophy of his victory, the Sphinx allows him to carry off her inert body with the mask of Anubis over her head. As he leaves, the gods appear in their true form, gigantic, veiled, irridescent. Their mysterious presence dominates the stage and casts its shadow on the eager young hero as he departs for his newly won kingdom.

The Sphinx and Anubis are pure inventions of Cocteau's. There is nothing of this sort in Sophocles. Their strange machinations help to give the play a fairy tale aspect. Francis Fergusson in his *The Idea of a Theater* says that it is "as though through the din of a cocktail party, he [Cocteau] were endeavoring in secret asides to tell a fairy story to a child." [3] The unity of this second act is not in the myth of Œdipe, nor in the fabricated intrigue. We must dig to another level where Œdipe becomes the fairy tale hero who slays the wicked monster and marries the princess. The princess, of course, is Mother, because the fairy tale hero is always, at least implicitly, a child. Many details reinforce this interpretation of the play as fairy tale. The use of the marvelous: the ghost of Laius, Anubis and the Sphinx, the final reappearance of Jocaste after her death. The dimensions of the platform minimize the epic scope of the myth. The actors are like children on a miniature stage. The flatness of the characterizations permits us to see Œdipe as the unique hero who is really a projection of the author's (and our) childish fantasy. The play might be called an improvisation on a fairy tale. Its real unity is in this simple make-believe dream tale, and from this center it extends to other levels.

Act III shows us the royal bedroom, "red like a little butcher shop amid the architecture of the city." The Voice announces: "Œdipe and Jocaste are finally alone in the nuptial chamber. They are asleep on their feet, and in spite of several polite hints from destiny, sleep will prevent them from seeing the trap which shuts on them for always." We are to witness the first minutes of an extraordinary marriage. The Voice announces it solemnly, but the action at times is light, almost whimsical. A deliberate ambiguity is maintained. We know that we are seeing something that should not be seen, and our empathy for the characters evokes in us repressed and forbidden emotions. The sleep into which Œdipe and Jocaste are on the verge of falling prolongs the stage "business" and attenuates the passion of the wedding night. By the use of such devices as Œdipe's cradle, with which Jocaste has never been able to part, the double role of the protagonists is kept present to the audience. Cocteau plays ironically on this double role in a deliberate act of provocation. By many subtle hints he continually reminds us that we are witnessing the honeymoon of a mother and son.

While Jocaste retires to prepare for bed, Œdipe receives an official visit from Tirésias. Œdipe is arrogant and insolent with the high priest. Tirésias tells Œdipe that the oracles are ominous, but Œdipe brags that he will outwit them.

TIRÉSIAS

Do you think that they can be outwitted?

ŒDIPE

I am the proof. And even if my marriage vexes the gods, what are you going to do about your promises, about your liberation, about the death of the Sphinx! and why have the gods pushed me on to this very chamber if this marriage displeases them?

TIRÉSIAS

Do you claim to resolve in one minute the problem of free will? Alas! Alas! your power intoxicates you.

Œdipe and Jocaste are finally alone.

This is not the only time that Cocteau has used the theme of incest. Here, as in *Les Parents terribles* and in the novel *Les Enfants terribles,* an incestuous situation is evoked without the full, conscious knowledge of the protagonists. I say without *full* knowledge because there is a kind of threshold awareness in both Jocaste and Œdipe. Jocaste says in Act I: "Little boys all say: 'I want to be a man so I can marry mother.' That isn't so stupid, Tirésias. Is there a sweeter couple, a couple sweeter and more cruel, a couple prouder of itself, than this couple, a son and a young mother?" And in Act III:

TIRÉSIAS

It is of that love, Œdipe, that I demand an explanation. Do you love the queen?

ŒDIPE

With all my soul.

TIRÉSIAS

I mean: Do you love to take her in your arms?

ŒDIPE

I love best that she take me in hers.

TIRÉSIAS

I compliment you on that nuance. You are young, Œdipe, very young. Jocaste could be your mother. I know, I know, you are going to reply—

ŒDIPE

I am going to reply that I have always dreamed of this kind of love, of an almost maternal love.

But compare this dim awareness with the terrible guilt of Racine's Phèdre, whose crime is of a far less serious nature. The psychology of the modern author is much less realistic. Although as highly nuanced, it does not stem from the perception of a basic truth. The characters are aware only of their peripheral emotions. Though they analyze these emotions with intelligence, their real psychological dilemma escapes them.

The remainder of the act is a succession of nightmares. As Œdipe begins to tell Jocaste a fictitious account of how he killed the Sphinx, she falls asleep. Then both sleep, and we see the dream of Œdipe. Anubis mockingly repeats Œdipe's boast: "Thanks to my sad childhood, I pursued studies which give me many advantages over the schoolboys of Thebes, and I don't imagine that this naïve monster expects to find himself face to face with the pupil of the best scholars of Corinth. But if you have played a trick on me, I'll pull your hair. (*Rising to a howl.*) I'll pull your hair, I'll pinch you till you bleed! I'll pinch you till you bleed!"

And Jocaste dreams the same terrible dream which she had told Tirésias in Act I: "I am awake, it is night; I rock a sort of baby. Suddenly, this baby becomes a gluey mess which runs between my fingers. I scream and try to throw away that mess; but—oh! Zizi! If you knew, it is foul—that thing, that mess, stays fastened to me, and when I think myself free, it bounds quickly back and strikes my face. And that mess is living. It has a sort of mouth which fastens on my mouth. And it spreads everywhere: It searches my belly, my thighs. What horror!"

They wake, and Jocaste removes Œdipe's tunic from his sweaty body:

JOCASTE

Come now! what a big baby! You mustn't be left in all that sweat. Don't make yourself heavy, help me.

ŒDIPE

Yes, my adorable little mother.

JOCASTE (*imitating him*)

Yes, my adorable little mother. What a child! Now he thinks I'm his mother.

ŒDIPE (*awakened*)

Oh, pardon me, Jocaste my love, I'm absurd. You see, I'm half asleep, I've mixed everything up. I was a thousand miles away, with my mother who always thinks I'm too cold or too hot. You aren't angry?

JOCASTE

Silly boy! Let me take care of you and go to sleep. Always excusing himself, begging my pardon. What a polite young man, my word! He must have been coddled by a very good Mama, too good, and now he leaves her, you see. But I have nothing to complain of, and I love her with all my lover's heart, the Mama who petted you, kept you, brought you up for me, for us.

ŒDIPE

You're so good!

JOCASTE

Tell me more. Your sandals. Lift your left leg. (*She takes off his shoe.*)

And your right leg. (*Same action. Suddenly she utters a terrible cry.*)

ŒDIPE

Did you hurt yourself?

JOCASTE

No—no. (*She draws back, looks at Œdipe's feet like a mad-woman.*)

ŒDIPE

Ah! my scars. I didn't think they were so ugly. My poor darling, were you afraid?

Once again, although they do not recognize it for what it is, their destiny whispers to them. The name Œdipe means Swollen Foot. Jocaste has discovered the wounds where Œdipe's feet were pierced before he was abandoned on the mountain. She explains her terror with a lie: One of her servants had abandoned a child, its feet pierced, on a mountaintop. So once more, out of their own weakness and blindness, Œdipe and Jocaste miss the opportunity to save themselves. A drunk cries outside the palace window, as a last crude warning:

Madame, whom are you fooling
Madame, whom are you fooling?
Your husband is too young
Much too young for you. . . .

But nothing can save them, and at last Œdipe falls asleep, while Jocaste sits beside him, stroking his head with one hand and with the other rocking the tiny muslin cradle.

Act IV is modeled on the form of *Œdipus Rex.* Much of it is taken directly from Cocteau's translation of Sophocles, which was not produced until after *La Machine infernale,* in 1937, at the Nouveau Théâtre Antoine. A messenger arrives to inform Œdipe of the death of Polybe, king of Corinth. Œdipe now learns for the first time that he is merely an adopted child. Tirésias and Jocaste try to persuade him not to search further, but he shows the same stubbornness which won him his high place. He is no longer the ambitious young man seeking fame and honor. He is the hero searching his own truth, at whatever cost. He is the Œdipus Rex of Sophocles. Jocaste hangs herself with the fatal scarf. No sooner has Œdipe faced this blow than he must turn to face another even more severe, the arrival of the shepherd who carried him, as a newborn infant, to the mountaintop:

ŒDIPE

Whose son am I, good man? Strike, strike quickly.

SHEPHERD

Alas!

ŒDIPE

I am near a thing impossible to hear.

SHEPHERD

And I—a thing impossible to say.

CRÉON

It must be said. I wish it.

SHEPHERD

You are the son of Jocaste, your wife, and of Laius, whom you killed at the triple crossroad. Incest and parricide, may the gods pardon you.

ŒDIPE

I killed him whom I should not have killed. I married her whom I should not have married. I perpetuated those whom I should not have perpetuated. All is made clear.

With this same cry, Sophocles' Œdipus leaves the stage to wreak vengeance on himself. So here; a moment later, he reappears, blood streaming from his eyes, accompanied by the child Antigone and the ghost of his dead wife.

The finale is infinitely touching and real. It is not vitiated by the presence of Jocaste, for the supernatural has established its rights early in the play. It is real because at this point and for the first time Cocteau has dramatized the tragedy of Œdipe, that tragedy which Sophocles, for the whole duration of *Œdipus Rex,* holds fixedly before the spectator. Cocteau's art up to this point has operated by a skillful process of selection, revealing subsidiary aspects of the story while leaving the great tragic truth in shadow. It lies there in the shadows, just beyond the reach of our skeptical modern minds, while we see the characters in roles that we can comprehend in our terms —the terms of ambition or flirtation or fantasy or anger. And then, when the situation has acquired the necessary degree of credibility, we see what we have known all along. Œdipe is a tragic hero. His doom is not merely an oracular play on words but social, moral and biological fact. The meaning of tragedy is ultimately obscure, but in Sophocles and in Cocteau it is dramatically real.

Cocteau's strategy here is sensitive and imaginative. He reconciles seeming opposites in an ingenious and convincing manner. We have a modern and an antique hero, a bedroom farce and a Greek myth. And the myth, seen through this screen of petty intrigue, assumes something like its old dimension. It extends beyond the narrow limits of the platform with its cardboard palace to strike reverberations in that racial conscience which poetry helps preserve.

In his study of *La Machine infernale,* Francis Fergusson makes the following important observation: The entire play, with the exception of the last act, shows us a diminished world, a world of light, boulevard comedy replete with suggestive plays on words and *double-entendre*. Mr. Fergusson sees the Thebes of these three acts as "any demoralized Balkan or Mediterranean commercial city of our time or any time." Œdipe is not the mythical scapegoat of the gods. He might be "the winner of a bicycle marathon or an ambitious politician who achieves the worldly *gloire classique* by stabilizing the franc for a day." [4] The treatment of Jocaste is largely comic. She is the type of extravagant woman to be found in the casinos of

Monte Carlo or in the most expensive loge at the Opera in Paris or Milan. Œdipe's meeting with the Sphinx is witty but almost meaningless repartee, such as might pass between a young man and young woman in a boulevard comedy. And the climactic wedding night flirts with the idea of incest just as the boulevard comedy flirts with the idea of adultery. Yet, and this is the point, there is all the terror and mystery of the universe just beyond the bedroom. Beyond the bedroom or drawing room of the boulevard comedy there is nothing but other bedrooms and other drawing rooms. Up until the last act, Cocteau operates by a process of suppression. What he says is important for what he leaves unsaid. The charming inconsequence of Jocaste or the male vanity and youthful enthusiasm of Œdipe are pathetically inadequate to cope with the terrible plot in which the gods have involved them. Even the meeting with the Sphinx has only the artificial terror of Grand Guignol. It is only in the fourth and final act that the play abruptly emerges into the mythic world of Sophocles.

Given this difference in dramatic strategy, we must expect important differences in the meaning of the tragedy as interpreted by the two authors. In the *Œdipus Rex* of Sophocles, the plot, as Mr. Fergusson says, is the search for a culprit, the search, that is, for the human responsibility which has brought on the plague which is decimating the city. As the search goes on, we see that it is not merely a search for the cause of the plague: ". . . the action which Sophocles shows is a quest, the quest for Laius' slayer; and . . . as Œdipus' past is unrolled before us his whole life is seen as a kind of quest for his true nature and destiny." [5]

Cocteau's Œdipe is not involved in such a quest until the final act. He is presented with tender irony, in Acts II and III, as an ambitious young man, naïve, vain, headstrong. He knows the odds are against him, but he doesn't care. Mr. Fergusson says that he is like a gambler. He wants to see if he can "beat the rap." As the play advances, there are many signs which tell Œdipe that he is doomed (just as the Voice, at the start of the play, tells us the whole story in advance), but Œdipe prefers to ignore these "polite hints from destiny." Œdipe is curiously blind. He refuses to see, until, in his literal blindness, he sees what should have been apparent all along. Œdipe is running away from that same truth that Sophocles' Œdipus is struggling to find. What, as Cocteau sees it, is that truth? And how may this obstinate refusal to see, to accept and to understand be interpreted?

What Œdipe refuses to see is what the title of the play tells us. The universe is a machine designed not for man's well-being but for his annihilation. The Voice tells the audience in the play's prologue: "Watch, spectator, rewound, so that its spring slowly uncoils for the length of a human life, one of the most perfect machines ever built by the infernal gods for the mathematical annihilation of a mortal man."

This view of nature as a hostile force is not unique to the *Machine infernale*. We can find expressions of this same view over and over again in Cocteau's other works. In *Journal d'un inconnu* he tells us that time is "a vibrating, rustling, terrifying immobility." We inhabit a universe without law where "that supreme justice proves to us at every moment that it acts according to an incomprehensible code which upsets our own, destroying the good, abetting the evil, doubtlessly in the name of some occult economy for which it does not want man to substitute himself. Nature causes us to destroy en masse." Man is simply "dust in a cyclone." And of Nature he says that she is "equally enamoured, it seems, of life and of murder; she thinks only of her belly and of pursuing an invisible task whose visibility demonstrates her total indifference to the sufferings of the individual." [6]

Nature, the universe which surrounds us and into which we are incorporated, is a vast machine which rolls unremittingly on without regard for the individual human destiny. Cocteau considers human society essentially hostile to the poet. This hostility is observable historical fact, and Cocteau's sensitivity to it might be interpreted as a Romantic survivance. But in the examination of this play, it is apparent that the view of society as hostile draws its force and cogency from a broader philosophical view. Tragedy, as Cocteau sees it, flows from man's precarious state in a universe which is not designed for him, a universe in which he is a mathematical nonentity caught in the machinations of a giant equation.

In the film *Orphée* the poet asks where the head bureaucrat of Hell can be found. Death replies: "He lives nowhere. Some believe that he thinks of us. Others that he thinks us. Still others believe that he always sleeps and that we are his dream—his bad dream." The world is a thought in the mind of a perhaps nonexistent God; history is a logical process which, however, shows no teleology, no creative evolution, no hope of the ultimate emergence of absolute mind or spirit. In this universe the last traces of divine providence or divine will have been abandoned in favor of an inexorable mechanism. Man, with his perpetual need for love, friendship and understanding, is doomed to be ground to bits in such a universe which treats him not as a person but as an object. Man can appeal to nothing beyond himself. His fellows, grouped into self-centered, defensive social units, are relentless enemies of the aspiring individual. Even freedom is of dubious value in this universe.

What can the individual do, caught as he is in this tragic impasse? What, in other words, is the conduct of a tragic hero? Cocteau's answer seems to be, in *Bacchus* at least, that the hero achieves the victory of failure. If he cannot control nature, he can at least control himself and, before he dies, triumphantly affirm his own dignity and power. The hero attempts to transcend the impersonal anonymous destiny which nature prepares for him. He rebels at the unmarked grave of time and marshals his forces for a great act of foolhardiness and daring which is doomed to triumphant failure: failure because man himself is in nature and cannot transcend it into, say, the timeless realm of Grace; triumphant because his audacity wins for him a mythological status in history and in the minds of his fellow men.

It is in the manner of this affirmation that Cocteau's heroes would seem to differ from the conventional tragic hero. Cocteau's heroes are invariably involved as sufferers. Theirs is largely a passive role. They are pursued and tracked down while battling to free themselves from society or from the forces of nature. These heroes choose only to be different from other men and women. But they do not choose any specific course of action. They lift up their heads proudly as destiny strikes them down, but not in the name of any cause or allegiance. To borrow a term from the vocabulary of Jean-Paul Sartre, they are not *engagés*.

We come now to the central problem in any criticism of Cocteau: the problem of liberty. Roger Lannes affirms at several points in his long essay on Cocteau that destiny and free will are Cocteau's central preoccupation. Cocteau himself has confirmed M. Lannes: "I was thus taken for erratic and dispersed while I turned and swung my lantern about in order to light from numerous angles different aspects of human solitude and of free will." [7] In other words, no matter what he might have seemed to be up to, Cocteau was in reality treating the themes of solitude and free will. This concern with the problem of liberty is most marked in those books which Cocteau has written since the end of World War II and the advent of Jean-Paul Sartre.

In France the meaning of liberty and its relation to life and literature have been brought most vividly into focus by Jean-Paul Sartre and the philosophers of Existentialism. The contact with Sartre and his works seems to have forced Cocteau to a reappraisal of his own position. Although he is in no way, as François Mauriac suggested, in his open letter to the *Figaro littéraire,* a disciple of Sartre, it seems likely that Sartre's Existentialism brought to Cocteau's mind some serious doubts about his own conception of liberty. Far from being a disciple of Sartre, Cocteau felt that he had to defend his own point of view against this persuasive man and doctrine. And while Cocteau may have settled these doubts to his own satisfaction, others may be less easily satisfied. It is in terms of the Existentialist theory of liberty that we shall see Cocteau's most serious failure as a playwright.

Cocteau indicates that his own conception of *engagement* differs from Sartre's in the following lines: "For one can be 'engaged' at all heights on the ladder. From the top to the bottom. Sartre is on the trail of something big there. But why does he limit himself to a visible engagement? The invisible engages us even further. Otherwise, this excludes poets who engage themselves with no other expectation than of losing. My detractors grant me a liberty which engages me—on false routes. I know what they are thinking of. Opium, police raids, and so on. What do opium and raids have to do with it? Our engagement is a thing of the soul. It consists in not leaving oneself an inch of comfort." [8]

This somewhat incoherent passage raises questions which Sartre himself has already answered. Sartre says, for instance, that the question of whether or not our actions may be crowned with success has nothing to do with the absence or presence of liberty. Thus, although it be assumed that a poet is always certain to fail in his endeavor, he is nonetheless free. The choice of the vocation of poet is itself a free choice. If Sartre has emphasized the "visible" forms of engagement, politics for instance, this does not mean that he excludes other meaningful relationships between man and himself. Indeed, engagement is first of all a private matter because it is the choice of ourselves through the way we choose to exist and the goals for which we choose to exist. Yet there is an important difference in the way in which these two writers envisage the choice of oneself. Cocteau points up this difference precisely when he says: "Sartre knows what I think of it [the theory of engagement]. My engagement is to lose myself in my most comfortless extremity. If I were to engage myself on the outside, either I would betray the exigencies of my inner engagement or those of my outward engagement." [9]

In a more recent essay, Cocteau reiterates this stand: ". . . my engagement was in myself and not exterior to me." Cocteau avers that he has remained faithful to himself rather than to any cause. His "morality" or responsibility consists in a tenacious adherence to an image of himself. "Engagement without faith is a sacrilege. I will never accept it. I am an anachronism. A free man." [10] Liberty here seems to be equated with what we have already denominated as "purity." This is no doubt the most fundamental meaning of purity as Cocteau envisages it— freedom from obligation, commitment, involvement, engagement, from anything which would distort or deform the poet's or hero's image of himself. Cocteau refuses commitment for the same reason that Sartre seeks it, that is, because of the shaping influence which a chosen course of action exerts upon the personality and the innermost being of the agent. Cocteau says that we must resist the pressure of the world around us which is constantly molding us, and, according to this view, destroying what is most personal and unique in us. As we have seen in examining *La Machine infernale,* we are persecuted by the forces of society and nature. Our freedom is strictly limited by our own weakness: "Our acts can do nothing, being ascribable to some current of air which rustles dead leaves."[11]

Freedom is further limited by our lack of control over destiny: "Free will and destiny are woven together. We tend to yield to destiny on the pretext that it has only a single visage. But it has several which contradict each other and complement each other like the double profile of Janus."[12] Victims of a cruel and inscrutable universe, our best course of action is a passive resistance or flight from any involvement which would catch us up in the machinery of the world and hence dehumanize us.

The world inspired Cocteau's characters with fear, although the fear is usually masked by bravado. Any kind of influence from the world outside or from other persons is felt as a threat to the character's very being. This fear arises, not from the contemplation of a course of action, not from the mustering of his spiritual and physical forces to control a situation, but rather from the apprehension of the situation. It is a kind of paralysis or, at best, flight from the situation.

Sartre makes this important distinction between fear and anguish: "We must agree with Kierkegaard: Anguish is distinguished from fear by this, that fear is fear of beings in the world and that anguish is anguish before myself. . . . Most of the time dangerous or menacing situations have several aspects: They will be apprehended through a sentiment of fear or of anguish depending on whether or not one envisages the situation as acting on the man or the man acting on the situation." [13]

Anguish in Sartre arises when we apprehend our freedom, when we realize, that is, that nothing justifies us and that we cannot justify ourselves. The thought that we must create and sustain our own values by continuous acts of choice causes an anguished awareness of responsibilities which we cannot avoid. We are locked in ourselves, yet condemned to act, unable to exist until we choose ourselves through the choice of a situation among other beings. We are a freedom which seeks to concretize itself by engaging itself in the world around it.

Sartre's conception of freedom differs from Cocteau's in two fundamental ways. The first is in the importance of the end or goal for which we act. Cocteau seeks to avoid commitment to an end at all cost, for this commitment would limit him and therefore "falsify" his personality. Sartre, on the other hand, believes that liberty exists only "in situation," that is, in a context of means, limits and possibilities determined by an end. Liberty does not choose what or how it will be; it chooses the end for which it will be: "Thus by its very projection toward an end, liberty constitutes as a being in the midst of the world a particular *datum* that it [liberty] has to be. It does not choose itself, for that would be to choose its own existence, but by the choice that it makes of its end, it causes it [the datum] to be revealed in such and such a way, in such and such a light, together with the discovery of the world itself." [14] So it is primarily by the choice of an end or goal that liberty constitutes itself in the world.

Sartre tells us furthermore—and this is the second important distinction between Sartre and Cocteau—that liberty is a negation of the already constituted Self. The act of choice abolishes the configuration of the Self as it existed prior to the act of choice. That which we choose becomes a denial of everything that solicits us, from within and without, which we do not choose: ". . . the upsurge of liberty is caused by the double 'nihilization' of *the being that it* [liberty] *is* and of the being in the midst of which it is." [15]

It is precisely this negation of the Self that Cocteau fears and that he refuses to accept. For Sartre, liberty is only the liberty to choose. Cocteau believes that liberty ceases to be liberty when it chooses; it is only liberty not to choose. So Cocteau's characters are suspended in time and space, unwilling to commit themselves to a goal or course of action, fearful of the consequences to the personality which follow such commitment. They do not "project" themselves into the world with a dynamism determined by their original project. They suffer from a paralyzing fear which makes flight the only possible course of action. These characters are specialists in the arts of flight and evasion. They talk themselves out of action. Their talk itself is a form of flight. Flight is no more than a ruse, a false solution to the dilemma of men caught in a hostile universe.

It is what Sartre would call a solution of "bad faith" or self-deception, operating purely as a psychological release and in no way solving the fundamental human dilemma: the need to act. No doubt Sartre would see this failure to act and to choose, or the choice of a verbal "flight of fancy," as itself a commitment, but a disastrous one, one which recognizes neither the to-be-realized liberty of the Self nor the moral obligations thrust upon the Self by the facts of existence.

Cocteau's plays have a strange suspended quality and are frequently lacking in dramatic conflict. Sartre's analysis of liberty is cogent and relevant here, since it is evident that Cocteau has tried to examine himself in terms of Sartrian Existentialism and to defend himself from possible criticism from that quarter. The validity of such criticism of Cocteau cannot stand or fall with Sartre, however. We may make the same general criticism in terms of the standards of vulgarized Aristotelianism which are generally applied to dramatic works. It is a commonplace to say that the basis of drama is conflict and that the basis of conflict is choice. The choice which X makes conflicts with the choice of Y. The ensuing dialectic by which X and Y seek to impose their wills on each other and work through to a dénouement is drama. It is difficult, if not impossible, to maintain the illusion of reality on the stage, to produce that dramatic context into which the spectator is drawn and involved, if the characters are not "in situation," committed, choosing and contesting the choices made by others.

There is dramatic conflict in Cocteau. But this conflict is often submerged or sidetracked while the play focuses on other considerations. Spectacle, fantasy, the fairy tale atmosphere, these are all skillfully handled concomitants of the intermittent drama of Œdipe's struggle with the gods. Œdipe scarcely realizes that his antagonists are the gods until Act IV, when it is already too late. Orphée and Eurydice have a very superficial relationship. They dispute like lovers in a boulevard comedy. And, as a matter of fact, the psychological involvement in Cocteau's plays (with the exception of *Les Parents terribles*) is generally no deeper than in the typical boulevard comedy, wherein relationships are highly static and conventionalized. Just as the characters are not committed to the world, to some cause or principle, so they are not committed to each other. In *Bacchus,* we have a hero who acts continually, but without purpose, or with no other purpose than to affirm his purity, that is, his lack of involvement.

It is the term "purity" which best characterizes Cocteau's moral and metaphysical position. Perhaps it is more fitting to reserve, with Sartre, the name "liberty" for the power of choice. Liberty must be liberty *for* something other than oneself, and it is precisely this liberty that Cocteau refuses to his characters. His characters seek their salvation within themselves in various ways. It is noteworthy that all of Cocteau's major characters are intensely lyrical. This is so because one of their chief havens of retreat from the world is "pure" poetry—poetry as far as possible detached from any prose context or real existential structure. In lyrical flights, such as those of the characters Renaud and Armide, the poet projects himself in the form of a verbal complex, as if his imagination were the world and he might find involvement in the images which are spun from his own head.

Cocteau sees the universe as a fearful and hostile place. But so does Sartre, who speaks of the Self as menaced, in danger, on the defensive. But these dangers cannot in any way destroy the essential freedom of the Self, nor can they cancel in any way the need to take a stand. Cocteau reacts differently to danger. I have suggested that the Sartrian term "bad faith" might be applicable to the behavior of Cocteau's characters. They take the stance and make the gestures of heroes, but they are like tragic actors practicing before a mirror. They never get out of the dressing room and onto the stage. They spend hours arranging their costumes, but they are afraid to soil these costumes by contact with reality.

To what degree does this defect vitiate Cocteau's theater? Miraculously, the plays remain, like some architectural triumph, a tower without a base. They become alive precisely through Cocteau's passionate involvement in himself and his anguished efforts to transcend that self toward some deeper, finer realm. They are products of a highly developed artistic consciousness. Their flaw is not their maker's alone. It is the cultural sickness of an age which lives by substitutes, by lies, and in spite of the unchanging human need for truth. It is an age to which we can apply Cocteau's paradox, which is the very definition of "bad faith": "I am a lie which always tells the truth." [16] His "truth" is the need to transcend himself; but it is a truth concealed by the "lie" of his posturing characters. Bad faith, although common to all but a few rare individuals, is nonetheless

mysterious. There is a disproportion between motive and act, the true motive always being concealed. The ambiguity of Cocteau's style and the purity of his heroes are functions of fear and the failure to become involved; because these aspects of his work are concealed by a brilliant masquerade, they are mysterious, that is, their true meaning and import are concealed. A lie, however, always ends by telling the truth, and the merit of Cocteau's heroes is the uncompromising anguish with which they live their lies.

Cocteau
as moralist

THE TRANSPOSITION OF MYTH INTO MODERN TERMS HAS NOW become a familiar method in modern literature. Joyce's *Ulysses* is of course the greatest example of this technique to be found in English literature. The plays of Giraudoux, Anouilh and Cocteau make use of myth in somewhat the same way as Joyce's novel. The play is first firmly anchored in the deep, permanent substratum of human experience, represented by the myth; then, against that substratum the playwright rings out the countless ironies which arise from the contrast with modern manners of feeling and speaking. In *Ulysses,* the fundamental irony is the contrast between the epic poem, with its heroes and heroines, its grandeur and its gods, and the benighted world of modern naturalism, the city-dweller reduced to the less than elemental, yet at odd moments the *Homo universalis,* potentially at least the dauntless hero, husband and voyager.

In *La Machine infernale* Cocteau is constantly searching for ironies which are generated by the contrast between the myth and the special dramatic tradition in which he has chosen to operate. The first three acts of the play are a kind of brilliant preparation in a minor key of comedy for Act IV in which the tragedy of Œdipus hits us with full dramatic force.

Cocteau seems to have worked on the justifiable assumption that a modern audience could not go along with the tragedy of Œdipus in all its primitive directness. And so he brings us to this tragedy indirectly, by pointing up comic overtones, sexual ambiguities or purely spectacular elements which would never have been dreamed of at the time of Sophocles but which are available in a modern perspective. And ultimately, despite all our modern skepticism, our refusal to believe in tragic action, destiny or human responsibility, we are drawn into the full tragedy of Œdipus and his family.

Myth is the world of the significant action, the large emotion. Myths have a certain credit; we believe that men used to believe in them, and hence we can watch the unfolding of a myth with a degree of hypothetical faith. Yet, even as the myth helps us believe in a world of significant action, it limits this belief; for myth represents a far greater remove from reality for us than it did for the Greeks. And thus we might expect to find a second and equally important use of myth in Cocteau's "poetry of the theater," based this time on the myth's *unreality*. Not only does Cocteau use the myth as a pretext for bringing large emotions into his plays; in each one he also introduces elements of fantasy which are suggested, or may be authorized in one way or another, by the myth: Death and the horse in *Orphée,* the Sphinx in *La Machine,* Ginifer and the talking flower in *Les Chevaliers de la Table Ronde.*

Cocteau's use of myth is therefore quite complex. While evoking a world of significant action and emotion, it serves, at the same time, as an ironical backdrop for the petty actions of modern man. Related to this ironical aspect is the use of myth to orient the play in a realm of fantasy, thereby undermining anything realistic in character or action. We find ourselves in a mysterious zone where things are real and unreal at the same time. This ambiguity is closely related to the inherent ambiguity of Cocteau's style. It is re-enforced by the constant juxtaposition of the commonplace and the marvelous, the ironic and the tragic, the banal and the lyrical. Myth frees the poetic imagination from the restrictions of reality and allows it to move with agility. Our remove from myth allows the poet even greater freedom. He can modify the myth as he chooses, without offense to the conservative popular imagination which has long since ceased to regard the myth as literally true.

Les Chevaliers de la Table Ronde is an important instance

of "poetry of the theater." It takes absolute liberty with its mythic sources. An important device of the play carries the paradox or ambiguity which is typical of Cocteau's method. This device centers around the character of Ginifer, who has the power of assuming the shape and form of anyone else. Hence we sometimes see the "real" personage, Gauvain or Guenièvre, and at other times the "false" Gauvain or Guenièvre as impersonated by Ginifer. Needless to say, the "real" and the "false" personages are played by the same actor. The very characters of the play are at once "real" and "false." And, as we shall see, it is not absolutely certain that the "real" characters are more real than their doubles. Such an ambiguity is in keeping with Cocteau's esthetic, his metaphysic, and with the general atmosphere of his plays.

This ambiguity is picked up and repeated by other elements of the play. But its chief correlative is the main conflict of the play, which is between truth, as represented by King Artus, and falsehood, as represented by Merlin. The play is ostensibly about the triumph of truth over falsehood, but it is a triumph which is highly qualified. This is of course what we should have expected from Cocteau; for he accords truth only a qualified belief. Truth, according to Cocteau, is within us. It is something we create out of the impossible contradictions and complexities of our interaction with the world.

Cocteau felt that he was breaking with a "kind of Grecian mania" by writing *Les Chevaliers de la Table Ronde,* a play suggested by the *matière de Bretagne,* the folklore romances of King Arthur and his followers.[1] Roger Lannes points out a number of similarities between *La Machine infernale* and *Les Chevaliers:* "Œdipe pursues the secret of his birth, just as Galaad rushes to the conquest of the Grail. Both pass through traps and trials, protected by the very thing which threatens them: destiny. Œdipe defies the Sphinx. Galaad arises unscathed from the chair of perils. From having lived a lie Jocaste dies as does Queen Guenièvre. When the truth bursts forth, with its august and definitive cruelty, Œdipe puts out his eyes, and Galaad is blind before that unbearable illumination." [2] Perhaps, in other words, Cocteau was still in the grip of his "Grecian mania."

M. Lannes does not mention, however, a crucial difference between the two plays. In *La Machine infernale,* and in *Antigone* and *Orphée* as well, the hero is presented largely as a sufferer. He is acted upon by the crushing forces of society or nature. The triumph of Œdipe and that of Galaad are different. Galaad, an almost magical figure, does not know "the victory of failure." The resolution of *Les Chevaliers* is much less anguished than that of *La Machine.* Artus and his knights find their own truth. They are not the playthings of the gods. And so the play (which was conceived during a night of feverish sickness) gives us a moment of peace and tranquillity, a state which Cocteau seems to have reached more and more often in his later years. The hallucinations of *Potomak* and *Opium* give way to the fantasy of *Les Chevaliers,* the lyricism of *Renaud et Armide* and the lucidity of *La Difficulté d'être.*

In *Orphée* Cocteau adapted a mythical plot, changing it almost entirely to suit his own ends. *La Machine,* while remaining faithful to the myth, shows a more complicated use of dramatic and literary devices. *Les Chevaliers* takes something from both of these plays. It equals *La Machine* in the use of spectacular visual effects and richness of language, while its plot is a sustained and original invention, capable of supporting the full weight of an elaborate spectacle and a large cast of characters.

It is in terms of this plot that Cocteau's development as a dramatic poet can be seen most clearly. There is something allegorical, reminiscent of the medieval mystery play, in the play's central struggle between good and evil. The play has great unity. From whatever angle we approach it, we are brought back to a moral struggle objectified in plot by the struggle of Merlin and the knights of King Artus. The plot, in other words, is a metaphor; this is one of the fundamental requirements of poetic drama.

Plot is a series of causally related events. These events, to a greater or lesser degree, embody in concrete terms the general idea that the play is trying to express. The degree to which plot is a metaphor might be considered the real criterion of plot. The variations of plot and subplots must be related, more or less schematically, to the more or less nuanced "statement" which the play attempts to make. The types of metaphor and metaphorical statement are, of course, very numerous. The degree to which meaning emerges, the way it emerges, the ironies and counter-ironies of plot, are infinitely various. But that there be a unified meaning and that it emerge through the plot seems to be the condition of drama, based on the nature of human psychology, on the directive and organizing role, that is, of reason in the psychic life.

The two central figures of Les Chevaliers, both of them venerable old men wielding great power, are Merlin and King Artus. Merlin seeks to create confusion and disorder—evil as Cocteau understands it. Artus, king in the world of men, tries to establish order, symbolized by the Grail, and drive evil out of his land. This central struggle is illuminated by three subplots. Indeed, the conflict of Merlin and Artus becomes realized only in the subplots. There is never a real confrontation scene between these two main figures of the play. The subplots mirror the main plot, thereby adding a level which is lacking in the latter. Each makes a different kind of commentary; and together they deepen the drama and the meaning of the play.

The main action revolves around the rather generalized conflict between Merlin, the power of evil, and Artus, the confused but worthy representative of good. At the start of the play, Artus' "impotence" is suggested. He is the fisher king whom modern anthropological critics are so fond of citing as the mythical prototype of the tragic hero. A curse lies on the land of Artus. The King himself is bewitched by Ginifer disguised as Gauvain. Ginifer, who is Merlin's valet—a kind of Scapin or Scaganarelle who continually gets himself and his master in and out of trouble—does not actually appear in the play. He is seen only in the guise of the various characters he impersonates—Gauvain, Galaad, Guenièvre. The actors must try to suggest a single personality through the different roles. This is facilitated by certain mannerisms and faults of pronunciation which distinguish Ginifer.

Everyone appears to be under a spell. Almost the first words that Lancelot, the paragon of courage, speaks to the Queen are, "I'm always afraid someone may hear us." And a little later he cries: "This castle no longer lives, it sleeps. This castle sleeps, and we are its dreams. Life is dead, dead, dead. In vain the sun of our love deceives you. Life is dead around us and perhaps because of us." (Act I) The symbol of this disorder is the loss of the Grail. The Grail symbolizes order, self-knowledge, truth. To the Queen's plea that he abandon himself to their love, Lancelot replies: "I don't have this privilege of women who invent the happiness that they desire. I require real happiness, a real love, a real castle, a real country where the sun alternates with the moon, where the seasons unroll in order, where real trees bear real fruit, where real fish live in the rivers and real birds in the sky, where real snow uncovers real flowers, where everything is real, real, real, true. I have had enough of this gloomy light, of these sterile countrysides, without day, without night, where only ferocious beasts and rapacious creatures survive, where the laws of nature no longer function." And so, in all these ways, the realm is subject to Merlin's evil power.

The relation of the subplots to the main plot is the key to the play's force and meaning. The first subplot, which forms a parallel with the main plot, concerns Lancelot and Guenièvre. As the lines quoted above indicate, Lancelot is unwilling to continue his adulterous relationship with the Queen. He cannot be happy in a love that is based on deception. There is an obvious thematic parallel here with the main plot. The conflict of Merlin and Artus is given a more human dimension in the moral struggle of the adulterous lovers.

The second subplot is the proving of Galaad and the search for the Grail. Artus calls his council together, and they sit at the Round Table to await the arrival of this new pretender to the title of "All Pure." In Act I Galaad appears and submits to the test of the "siège périlleux." But first, Artus pronounces the ritual: ". . . And things heavy will become light and things light will become heavy and the Grail will cease to be an enigma and the meaning of what was obscure will be deciphered and spirit will dominate matter and the dragons will die and will spread their tongues upon the sand and truth will emerge forthright from its covering of sloth and enchantment." The lines have an almost Biblical cadence. In this play, as in *La Machine infernale,* Cocteau is close to making a kind of theological statement. He is always on the boundary of myth, theology or moral philosophy, although he does not at any time commit himself to a real position on these matters. The events of the play have the obscurity of folklore or myth. They rehearse more than they demonstrate or explain. They retain, in other words, the essential ambiguity of metaphor.

Galaad takes his place at the Round Table, thus proving his merit. He is the long-awaited "All Pure" who will drive the unclean spirit out of the land. In Act III, Cocteau tells us that Galaad is really the "poet." This interpretation is probably not as arbitrary as it seems; all Cocteau's heroes are poets. The essential heroism, for Cocteau, is the act of poetic creation.

To save himself, Merlin sends the knights off on a wild goose chase after a false Grail. They meet in an enchanted castle, where Lancelot plays chess with the devil, and finds and releases the true Gauvain. There is a highly comic scene in which Lancelot is brought to the verge of despair by the linguistic slips and shoddy behavior of Ginifer, disguised as the Queen. At the end of Act II, Merlin "rides" Ginifer, still in the form of the Queen, in order to hasten back from the castle to Artus' court. The effect of this scene is comic and a little frightening:

MERLIN (*mounting the false Queen and grasping her tresses like reins*)

Five and five do not make ten
In the name of the monkey and the son
In the name of the salamander
By flame and by cinder
Through the valley and the mountain
  May the queen be a horse

(*He repeats without stopping, at the rhythm of a gallop, this last line.*)

May the queen be a horse
May the queen be a horse

* * *

THE FALSE QUEEN (*shrieking*)

Let go! Let go! Watch out! Help! Pity, pity! My bones crack! He's pulling out my hair! I'm burning! I'm dying! Have pity on me! Help!

(*Still reciting the last line of the formula, Merlin seems to gallop, pulling the tresses with one hand and whipping his mount with the other. The tempestuous wind of the end of the First Act rises. Shadows and flashes. The walls fly away.*)

In the final act, Artus discovers that Lancelot and Guenièvre are lovers. He kills the knight, and this causes the death of Guenièvre, for she wills to die and is carried off by the fairies. But they are resuscitated in the land of the fairies and no doubt live there happily ever after. Even death is not serious in this play. There is something of the magic tranquillity of Shakespeare's *Tempest*. In Act III Galaad exposes Merlin. Finally the Grail appears. Everyone sees it but Galaad: "I will never see it. I am he who makes it visible to others." Sunlight and happiness are restored to the realm. The birds begin to sing and Ségramor, the son of Lancelot and Guenièvre, translates their message: "They say: Pay, pay, pay, pay, pay, pay, pay. You must pay, pay, pay." Only, that is, if we accept our responsibilities will the spell be lifted from our land and lives.

Cocteau is implying here the moral attitude of *La Difficulté d'être* and *Journal d'un inconnu*. The conception of self-knowledge as the basis for action is very old, but the orientation which Cocteau gives this theory (especially in his emphasis on the seemingly perverted or abnormal) suggests that he has been somewhat influenced by psychoanalysis with its relativistic approach to human behavior. Cocteau believes that we must know ourselves and accept responsibility for what we are. Morality consists in accepting this truth about ourselves, no matter what penalty society may impose on us. But there is danger of a contradiction here: Morality, conceived in this light, may very well produce confusion and disorder, the very things that Cocteau denominates as evil in this play. As we shall see in *Les Parents terribles,* truth—human truth—may often be a kind of disorder. Disorder may be creative and fertile while order is sterile and deadly. Obviously disorder cannot be both good and evil at the same time. It cannot, that is, unless we distinguish between two types of disorder: the pure and the impure. Such a distinction is not made in this play. But the contradiction is eased by another means: the use of irony and ambiguity arising out of the Ginifer plot. The other device, the distinction between pure and impure disorder, is employed in *Les Parents terribles.*

The search for the Grail (the Galaad plot) takes up much of the play. It allows the characters to change rapidly from place to place and undergo a series of adventures. Yet this subplot too makes its contribution to the metaphor of good and evil. It lends a dynamic quality to the play; it is, in fact, the pretext for most of the play's events. It is the search for the Grail, even more than the finding of it, which breaks the enchantment of Merlin. It is a search which, we finally realize, need not take place over great distances and in strange lands. Each one of us must search within himself. Thus the final lifting of the spell and the manifestation of the Grail takes place in King Artus' own chambers. The search plot also broadens the main theme and links up the characters with the theme, because each one of them, for one reason or another, wishes to search for the Grail.

The rebellion of Ginifer against his master is the third sub-plot. The comedy is very broad, often burlesque: for instance, Merlin's ride on the back of the false Queen. We have here a kind of parody of the main plot which, as it were, answers our criticisms and doubts about the probability and significance of that action. Cocteau has said that Ginifer is the main character of the play. Hence we are justified in giving his numerous parodies an important part in our analysis of the play. The other characters, such as Gauvain, are pompous and almost unreal in their adherence to the code and morals of chivalry. Ginifer, on the other hand, is an appealing scamp. He touches us more directly and seems, in a way, more real than the characters he impersonates, just as the Beast in Cocteau's film *La Belle et la bête* is more appealing and more real than the Prince.

The Ginifer parody operates by supplying a criticism of the play which at once expresses and contains our own skepticism. Ginifer is a device for poking fun at these pompous and simple-minded knights and ladies with their high moral purpose and their quest for truth. Ginifer also parodies the evil represented by Merlin. Hence he casts a limited but effective shadow of doubt on the struggle between truth and falsehood which the play portrays. No one is either as good or as bad as he pretends to be. Ginifer's presence insinuates that confusion is not entirely bad, order not entirely good. Human nature, Cocteau seems to be saying, is obstreperous, vulgar and irrational, like the character Ginifer. Not only does Ginifer imitate all the characters; perhaps, in a deeper sense, they really are Ginifer more than they are themselves. Every man's truth is in reality protean, changing and complex.

So the Ginifer parody does for the theme of the play what the extra-dramatic interventions of *Orphée* and *La Machine infernale* (the prologue and the "signature" of Cocteau's own name in *Orphée,* the Voice in *La Machine*) do for the dramatic illusion in those plays. There is a double irony at work which increases the play's credibility while seeming to deny it. Ginifer seems to poke fun at the struggle of good and evil; and yet, he represents a kind of skepticism which has to be expressed before it can be discounted. The play seems less naïve because of this added perspective. We are able to take its message more seriously.

Cocteau tells us in his preface that it is a matter of complete indifference to him that what is conventionally held as good seems to triumph in the end. It is a coincidence for which he renounces all responsibility. He would like, it seems, to identify himself exclusively with Ginifer. Yet is it not precisely because they have discovered the truth about themselves that Blandine and Gauvain are reunited; that Ségramor's wound is healed; that Galaad goes off to new adventures; that Lancelot and Guenièvre live happily ever after under the lake? These changes indicate that purification through self-knowledge is possible.

The theme of self-knowledge as a condition for happiness is found in even more highly metaphorical form in the film *La Belle et la bête*. Beauty discovers that she loves a monster; when finally she tells him of her love, he becomes physically beautiful, as if to prove that beauty, like truth, is a completely relative matter. The Beast is the only truly moral character in the film, because he knows that he is a monster. He becomes physically beautiful at the end of the film because moral beauty, which is nothing but self-knowledge, is the only true beauty.

In *Les Chevaliers,* Cocteau seems to say, through the ending of his play, that when this condition of self-knowledge is fulfilled, true happiness is possible. His subsequent denial of this possibility, in the preface, would seem to be a partial retraction of the ostensible theme of the play and a re-emphasizing of the element of skepticism expressed through the Ginifer plot.

Eight years later, in *La Belle et la bête,* Cocteau gave his film fairy tale a similar happy ending. Are we to conclude that happiness, tranquillity and peace seem to have appeared to Cocteau, as to the aging Shakespeare, to have become a mortal possibility? Certainly the purest joy to be found in any of Cocteau's works lies in his re-creation of that unattainable world which he describes, in speaking of *La Belle et la bête,* as the "lustral bath of childhood." [3] But happiness is to be found only in the re-creation of a lost childhood or in the mythic adventures of fantasy. Each image of this film is framed for the viewer as the fable itself is framed, in enchantment and wonder and lore. The camera-work situates the film in that area of imagination where we half believe the impossible, where metaphor is normal speech and miracle is a deeper truth than nature. Cocteau has created, in visual terms, an ageless atmosphere of wonder: the Beast's enchanted castle, the forest as alive as the animals which the Beast hunts and devours within it, the garden with the fatal rosebush from which the merchant plucks a rose to bring to his daughter, the beautiful white horse Magnifique, the magic glove and the magic mirror.

Works of such compelling fantasy as *La Belle et la bête* and *Les Chevaliers de la Table Ronde* seem to be a denial of man's quest for happiness in the world of reality, rather than an affirmation of its feasibility. Six years after *Les Chevaliers,* after a return to the harsh world of prose, neurosis and human conflict (*Les Parents terribles*), Cocteau revived another myth of enchantment and magic. *Renaud et Armide* is the apotheosis of a poet's search for peace and love through the operation of pure imagination. But here there is no fairy tale ending. The lovers do not soar off into the sky to live happily ever after. Fantasy, after all, is restricted to the narrow confines of an enchanted island: "In the end, everything works out, except the difficulty of being, which does not work out." [4]

All of Cocteau's expository writings show a strong concern with moral issues. *Opium, La Difficulté d'être* and *Journal d'un inconnu* return endlessly to questions of human behavior and motivation, the relation of the individual to society, the relative merits of action and contemplation and the problem of value. Cocteau has the clarity of style of the seventeenth century *moralistes*—Pascal, La Bruyère, La Rochefoucauld—and the abstract essentializing type of intellect so typical of the post-

Cartesian tradition. The cultural framework in which he operates, however, is the expressionistic idealism of the 1920's. His efforts to re-establish a moral issue are in contradiction to the very nature of his chosen frame of reference.

Les Chevaliers de la Table Ronde is expressionistic in form and conception, but its theme is the search for a kind of moral truth. While remaining faithful to his conception of man as essentially mysterious—hence, uncommitted and amoral—Cocteau tries, nevertheless, to come to terms with those more classical notions of human behavior which no Frenchman can ever entirely ignore. Although he cannot conceive of morality as the finding of one's place in a structured Cartesian universe, nor even, in the manner of Sartre, as the development of a personal relationship with a subjectively conceived universe, he dramatizes the search for these solutions.

The quest for the Grail leads the knight-errant beyond the quest for the truth of his own nature; he must also search for the meaning of life and establish values on the ruins of historical contradiction. The myth, which casts a ritual light on the quest, helps to situate it between the present and the past; while the form of the play is expressionistic, we often hear the *moralistes* as a kind of echo in the tone of Cocteau's words and in his syntax which tends inevitably toward antithesis and epigram. Galaad, whom Cocteau calls the poet, is mysteriously handicapped by his role as mediator and can never find the Grail himself. However, he helps others to find it by demonstrating the first and oldest of all moral imperatives—Know Thyself.

Neurosis
and naturalism

THE NATURALISM OF *Les Parents terribles* IS QUITE DISTINCT from the rather special theory of realism which Cocteau developed in his early works, although there is a definite link between them. Cocteau asserts that in the ballet *Parade* he employed "the Picassian method of the truer than the true (synthesis of familiar gestures into a dance)." [1] Because of this, that is, the use of the commonplace and familiar, *Parade* was called a "realistic" ballet.

In *Parade* Cocteau attempted, for the first time, to negate the dandyism of his early works, *La Lampe d'Aladin* and *Le Prince frivole.* Much of the detail of the ballet is directly imitated from street life, household noises and music hall numbers. However, these realistic elements are parodied and caricatured, not only in performance, but by opposition to the very theme of the ballet. The ballet tells us that the real truth of an event or a spectacle is something mysterious, that it takes place, in the words of the Managers, "on the inside." The parade is a mere caricature of a hidden tragedy. "Every living work includes its own parade. Those who do not enter, see only that parade. But the surface of an original work shocks, intrigues, irritates, the spectator too much for him to enter. He is repelled from the soul by the visage, by the novel expression which distracts him like a clown's grimace at the door." [2]

This use of realistic detail, which Cocteau attributes here to Picasso, actually derives from Baudelaire and Guillaume Apollinaire. Realism in these poets is always a means to some kind of total vision. So they express, for instance, the "doubleness" of reality through their use of metaphor or analogy. These figures of speech teach us that things not only exist for themselves but may also "stand for" intimate emotional states.

Or there may be a kind of sudden emotional connecting-up, as in the following quotation from Baudelaire, in which the vision of the city leads to a semi-mystical experience: "Religious drunkenness of great cities. —Pantheism. I am all of them; they are all me. Whirlwind." [3] Or finally, the poem may simply reveal to us an unexpected pathos and humanity in the apparently dehumanized life of the city. The poems of Apollinaire offer many examples of this direct use of realism. Even here, however, there is always a certain degree of symbolization and often deformation. Things are insisted upon as *representations* rather than as entities in themselves. They are, in other words, a parade which, if we are not careful, will conceal from us the deeper truth behind the spectacle. In this sense, all of Cocteau's works are realistic. Even when most personal and most eccentric or even when most obscure, they always refer back to observed reality. In the works which we have discussed up to this point, it is clear that the personal deforming vision predominates over the observed event.

Beginning with *Les Parents terribles,* however, Cocteau reversed his emphasis. Here the outer or objective aspect of realism predominates to such an extent that we must call this play, and the two that follow it, naturalistic.

Cocteau was led to make this change, in part, by his desire to conform to the laws of genre. The idea was not new. As early as 1917, the year of *Parade,* Raymond Radiguet influenced Cocteau along these lines. "We must write books as everybody else does," he said.[4] Radiguet's two novels seem to indicate that he meant that the traditional genres should be respected.

With *Les Parents terribles* in 1938, Cocteau seems to have attempted to incorporate his art and his message in the traditional genres. *Les Parents terribles* has been called a "vaudeville" by some critics,[5] and it and *Les Monstres sacrés* (1940) are vehicle plays, or *œuvres de circonstance. La Machine à écrire* (1941) is a detective play. *Renaud et Armide* (written in 1941, produced in 1943) is a classical verse tragedy. *L'Aigle à deux têtes* (1946) is Romantic melodrama à la Hugo. In these plays, myth and "poetry of the theater" are partially (sometimes entirely) absent. Cocteau, in other words, had departed radically from the very personal conventions which he had developed in his early plays and which the public, or at least a part of it, had learned to accept.

We might list a number of reasons for the use of the naturalistic convention in *Les Parents*. A tentative explanation might be an increased desire on Cocteau's part to communicate, to speak to the public out of a familiar context; perhaps then, by the use of this familiar context, making his own highly personal message more unequivocal. There was also the desire to write a play in which Jean Marais might play a typical young man of this day and age. And there was, as Cocteau tells us in his second preface, the desire to do away with "excess" of all sorts. Cocteau is referring here, in part, to that very "poetry of the theater" which seemed to come from the spectacle rather than the action and for which he had been criticized—for example, the talking flower and the chess game of *Les Chevaliers de la Table Ronde*.

These various motives, taken in conjunction with Cocteau's long-standing sense of realism, provide a kind of explanation for Cocteau's naturalism. But the very lack of relationship among these reasons suggests that the convention was not altogether suited to Cocteau's needs as an artist. The choice of a convention or genre cannot be arbitrary. Rather there must be a "marriage" of that convention with the playwright's deepest emotions, his values and his sense of language. There must be, in other words, a revaluation and a resituation of the playwright's themes, necessitated—and achieved—by the adoption of a new form.

Roger Lannes considers *Les Parents terribles* to be Cocteau's best play. I reserve my own opinion until the end of the chapter. But certainly it can be said to Cocteau's credit, at this point, that the rigor of the naturalistic convention was something he was prepared to meet; for his more poetic writings have a discipline and a rigor of their own.

Les Parents terribles had the reception usually accorded to a masterpiece: It was first refused by Louis Jouvet, who did not think it could succeed. Produced by Roger Capgras at the Ambassadeurs, *Les Parents* ran for two hundred performances before full houses. The Conseil Municipal de Paris intervened at this point and refused to allow an "incestuous" play to continue in a theater belonging to the city. Transferred to the Bouffes Parisiens, the play continued to run for another two hundred performances with its original cast—Germaine Dermoz, Alice Cocéa, Gabrielle Dorziat, Marcel André and Jean Marais. In 1941, when the play was revived at the Gymnase, disturbances were organized in the theater, and Cocteau was subjected to a concerted attack in the press. It was at this time that Jean Marais beat up a Collaborationist newspaperman named Alain Lambreaux. The actors resisted the nightly disturbances until a veritable riot, organized by elements of the fascist *Parti Populaire Français,* provoked the police into closing the theater. Vichy ordered it reopened. The Germans forbade any further performances of *Les Parents terribles*. Cocteau at last had achieved his great scandal; he had joined the ranks of Racine, Molière and Hugo.

The character of Yvonne, originally conceived for Yvonne de Bray, dominates the written text of *Les Parents*. The actor Jean Marais dominated the production before the footlights. Cocteau's friendship with Jean Marais represents that kind of collaboration between playwright and actor which often proves so fertile for the theater—in recent years rivaled only by Jean Giraudoux and Louis Jouvet. Cocteau's love of the theater and "minor beauty" found its focus and intensity in the person of the young actor who has become one of Cocteau's most successful "creations." Apprentice for a brief time with Charles Dullin at the Atelier, Jean Marais auditioned for Cocteau and was given the role of the chorus in *Œdipe-Roi* in 1937. Henceforth Marais starred in each new play of Cocteau's. The most important of these was *Les Parents terribles*. Indeed, Marguerite Jamois had told him: "You will never play any other role!" [6] With the overnight success of *Les Parents,* Marais became a star. After the defeat of France and his demobilization he appeared in the movies and, for a time, was a member of the Comédie-Française.

Acts I and III of *Les Parents terribles* are set in Yvonne's bedroom, the *chambre de meurtre* in which Cocteau situates his naturalistic monologues *La Voix humaine* and *Le Bel Indifférent,* that same room which he evokes in other books as the rendez-vous of tragic or forbidden love. The disorder of this room explains the name which the family give to their apartment. It is a *roulotte,* a little gypsy wagon on wheels. Its mobility suggests that they carry their disorder with them even outside the room. This dark, disorderly bedroom is not the coquettish and somehow sterile bedroom of a Feydeau vaudeville where the action is so febrile that no one has time to make love, nor is it Bernstein's bedroom of a *femme de goût.* Neither is it the bedroom of *La Machine infernale* beyond which we feel all the mystery and terror of the universe. It is the bedroom of naturalism; and beyond it there are only other bedrooms and other dramas much like the one that is about to be unfolded.

Pierre Brisson in his *Le Théâtre des années folles* describes Bernstein's technique as the "épisode-sursaut à triple décrochement," [7] that is, the play opens with a surprise, followed by three peripeties in the three acts of the play. And *Les Parents terribles,* which has often been compared to a work of Bernstein, follows this formula.

The opening *coup de théâtre:* Yvonne, who is diabetic, has nearly killed herself with an overdose of insulin. She is frantic with worry over her son Michel, who has not returned home that night. Yvonne loves her son passionately and exclusively. As a result, Georges, her husband, has taken a mistress. Léonie, Yvonne's sister, has always been in love with Georges. Léo, however, is not dominated by her passion. She is the voice of reason who explains the characters to themselves and chides them for their shortcomings. She watches the tragedy approach, influencing the other characters and guiding them. She is like two people. On the one hand she is the voice of reason and on the other a frustrated old maid who missed her chance for happiness out of a false sense of dedication to her sister. Michel finally returns home, radiantly happy. He is in love with a young woman; he has spent the night with her. His mother's fierce jealousy puts an end to his happiness. The act ends with the revelation that Michel's fiancée is also his father's mistress: "décrochement" or peripety number one. This twist of plot, by the way, is the chief similarity with boulevard comedy or vaudeville.

In Act II, the family goes to meet Michel's young sweetheart, Madeleine. He considers it a friendly family visit, but their intention is to break up his romance. Georges does this by threatening to reveal the truth to Michel if Madeleine does not repudiate her young lover. She does so by telling Michel that she has another lover. Michel leaves in despair. This second "décrochement" or peripety closes the second act. But Léo, who has been the guiding spirit of the intrigue, intervenes at this point with a word of hope. She has taken a liking to Madeleine and has decided to help her. In Act III, the young lovers are brought together again; but Yvonne, who has lost her son, makes another suicide attempt. This time she succeeds. So we have the third peripety which brings us back to the "épisode-sursaut" with which the play began.

Three sets of terms, which recur frequently, point to the meaning of the play, "order-disorder," "pure-impure," "children-grown ups." Cocteau says in his preface: "Two roles form the equilibrium of the order and the disorder which motivate my play. The young man whose disorder is pure; his aunt whose order is not." [8] Again we see Cocteau as the enemy of society; the praise of disorder, whether on the moral or political plane, is one of his most persistent themes. In his *Lettre aux Américains* he says proudly: "France is perpetually in conflict with herself. . . . The great French tradition is a tradition of anarchy. It is the most solid of all. Disorder allows France to live, just as order is indispensable to other peoples." There are several "great French traditions," of which the most celebrated —the tradition of Richelieu and Louis XIV, of Boileau and Racine—is not a tradition of anarchy. The point here, however, is not whether Cocteau is right or wrong but rather the meaning of this statement in terms of his own work and thought. This anarchy is like the essential nonconformism of the poet. Hence anarchy and disorder are creative: "I have often written that the spirit of creation is nothing other than the spirit of contradiction in its highest form." [9] And love, like creation, is another product of disorder.

Léo, who represents the sterile order which can be achieved in the absence of love, describes the disorder of love to her sister, who is not even aware that she inhabits a *chambre de meurtre*. She tells Yvonne that Michel has spent the night with a woman, that Georges has taken a mistress and that Yvonne's relationship with her son is selfish and dangerous. This is love, but it is love as a disorder. In Act I, scene 2, Léo compares it to crime: "I was telling you about crimes that one can commit unwittingly. There are no simple souls. Any country priest will tell you that the smallest village hides instincts of murder, incest and theft such as one doesn't find in the cities. No, I wasn't treating you like criminals. On the contrary! An authentic criminal nature is sometimes preferable to that semidarkness which you enjoy and which frightens me."

Cocteau has often compared human nature, with its carefully hidden mysteries, to the more open amorality of plants and animals. Part of his hostility to society comes from the fact that society prevents us from being ourselves, from accepting our peculiarities or abnormalities. In a criticism of Freud, Cocteau makes the point that we must embrace our disorder: "He [Freud] never consecrated the abnormal as a form of transcendence. He did not acclaim the great disorders." [10] These sentences, which have a decidedly Sartrian ring, are an attack on the bourgeois conception of normality and a fearful conformism. Love is the highest expression of the individual. It can exist only when the individual chooses to be himself rather than like others.

Léo also defines the kind of person in whom this disorder is found: "In this world there are children and grown-ups. I count myself, alas, among the grown-ups. You—Georges—Mik, you belong to that race of children who never cease to be the same, who would commit crimes—" These childlike people live in such a state of moral disorder that certain crimes mean nothing to them. So Yvonne thinks nothing of attempting to destroy Michel's happiness in order to keep him for herself. When she cannot do this, she destroys herself. Georges shows the same kind of selfishness in his desire to keep Madeleine. He even forces her into telling a degrading lie. Crime is as natural to these characters as it is to the Marquis de Sade, Maldoror or Querelle de Brest. Like these personages, Cocteau's characters illustrate a kind of Nietzschean morality which is to be arrived at through crime or disorder.

However, all disorder is not equally "moral." Disorder may be generous and creative, or it may be selfish and destructive. The distinction is made for us in this play by the dramatic conflict. That is, our sympathies are oriented toward Michel and Madeleine rather than toward Yvonne and the family. It would seem, then, that there are different types of disorder. Disorder, in fact, may be pure or impure. Purity corresponds to the character's freedom from involvement. We are free when we choose to adhere to an image of ourselves rather than something which solicits us from outside ourselves. The child and the criminal are both examples of *pure* disorder.

This play carries us one step further than *Les Chevaliers de la Table Ronde,* which recounts the triumph of order over disorder. In that play the author tries subtly (through a parody) and openly (through the preface) to discount the triumph, as if he were not altogether comfortable with it. And the fact of the matter is that Cocteau is not eager to see order always triumph over disorder. The very stuff of life would suffer in consequence—the richness, the complexity, the real truth of life which lies in its obdurate resistance to any kind of regimentation. The problem is solved in *Les Parents terribles* in another way. It is a way which offers obvious dramatic possibilities. The characters are aligned along thematic lines: One represents order, another "pure" disorder, and so on. Thus Cocteau is able to dispense with the parody, which would not have been so readily available in the naturalistic form. The plot itself has sufficient subtlety to give the necessary perspective and the irony which are vital to the dramatic illusion, without recourse to parody.

Dramatic conflict arises when pure characters come into conflict with other characters who have a stake in the order of things. In *Les Parents terribles* it is quite clear that we must sympathize more wholeheartedly with Michel and Madeleine than with the family. Michel is purer than his mother because he is less committed; he does not have as great a stake in the family. His purity comes easier. Furthermore, Yvonne's love for Michel has incestuous overtones which we are obviously expected to condemn. And yet why must we condemn them?

Although a condemnatory attitude is definitely suggested by the play, Cocteau, speaking as a critic of his own work, disclaims this intention. He says in his preface: "I have pushed as far as possible an attitude which is proper to me: that of remaining exterior to the work, defending no cause and not taking sides." But he seems to do precisely this; his sympathy for the young people is like an echo of Gide's cry: "Familles, je vous hais!" The impact of *Les Parents terribles* comes from the brutal frankness with which it reveals the pathology of what might be a fairly typical bourgeois family. The purity which Cocteau defends represents all that is youthful, innocent, uncivilized. The impurity (and also the order of which he speaks) is that static social system from which Cocteau himself emerged and against which he has always felt it necessary to defend himself.

This almost automatic preference for young people, the tendency to see adults as enemies, as the hated representatives of bourgeois society, may be explained by reference to Cocteau's "angelism." In his enthusiastic descriptions of his angel-heroes, Cocteau seems anything but objective. He views them with a scarcely hidden pride and tries to justify all the things that differentiate them from ordinary men. The poet too is an "angel." It seems clear that Cocteau, in describing these angels, is also describing himself: "Disinterestedness, selfishness, tender pity, cruelty, suffering caused by contact, purity in debauchery, mixture of a violent taste for earthly pleasures and scorn for them, naïve amorality. —Make no mistake: These are the signs of what we call angelism. It is possessed by any true poet, whether he writes, paints, sculpts or sings." [11]

Angels reappear frequently in Cocteau's poetry. Dargelos, the young tough of *Les Enfants terribles,* is an "angel." In a long development on angels in *Journal d'un inconnu,* Cocteau calls them "gracious, cruel, terribly male and androgynous monsters." [12] And later in the same pages, he describes his struggle with the "angel" of inspiration during the writing of *Orphée.* The "angel" for Cocteau may be a poetic symbol into which he projects some element of himself, or it may represent the homosexual partner who reproduces the poet's own boyhood and therefore is another self. Or it may be a cruel and fascinating young *voyou* such as Dargelos, himself a schoolmate of Cocteau's. There are some surprising angels in Cocteau's paradise. Jean Genet, the poet of murder, theft and homosexuality, would no doubt be among them. Cocteau once appeared in court as a character witness for Genet and stated that he was the "greatest living French writer." The nostalgia for childhood, the attitude of childhood and the attraction of young men who have somehow never grown up form a persistent theme in Cocteau. And this special psychological orientation seems to have influenced many of his works. It accounts, in part, for his hostility to society and the rather surprising assumption that children are more "moral" than adults.

This brand of "angelism" is related to the other, that is, the flight into the purity of hermetic lyricism. Cocteau's angels may reach their apotheosis in two ways. They may permit themselves to be destroyed by the world, or they may "destroy" the world by a poetic negation. Homosexuality, persecution, pure poetry, are the three phases of the dramatic movement which operates in all of Cocteau's works under various disguises. The themes are transmuted and subdued in the present play; but we are in the world of naturalism. Later, we shall return once more to the world of poetry and hyperbole where, despite the disguises of metaphor—or perhaps because of them —we shall see Cocteau's *tragique* in its ultimate form.

The play, as I have explained it here, would seem to be a defense of disorder. But the form in which Cocteau has couched his manifesto is the most orderly of all genres: the well-made play with its tidy machine-like plot. This contrast between substance and form provides a strong and creative irony. From it springs the deepest meaning which we can assign to the play. Do we not have here, in radically different terms, the theme of *La Machine infernale*? The characters are caught up in a "plot" against which they struggle blindly in the attempt to affirm their own unruly individuality. Here, the machine-like plot is the symbol of the implacable destiny ("plot" in a different sense) woven by the infernal gods. By a happy turn of events, Michel escapes this destiny. He is spared the horror of marrying his mother. But ultimately it is not his own strength or courage which saves him. It is mere chance and the unexpected and rather arbitrary pity of his aunt. The genre demands a happy ending. But our knowledge of Cocteau's philosophy suggests that it might just as well have been otherwise.

It even seems likely that Michel and Madeleine themselves will eventually become "parents terribles"; the same patterns will reassert themselves, the same struggle between order and disorder—a struggle which is the very essence of life itself—will blind them to their own limitations, lock them in upon themselves, and eventually cause them to produce the same suffocating and restrictive atmosphere from which Michel, Cocteau's typical young man, was himself forced to break away. The intricate plot constantly brings the characters face to face with themselves, producing a system of interlocking tensions and an atmosphere of anguish; there is no way out, unless it be the acceptance of the contradictions of family love and loyalty. Yet the truth, and hence the possibility of growth, are concealed from Michel; like all of Cocteau's heroes, he is a victim; and the conclusion of the play points to the ultimate irony of domestic tragedy—the victims will themselves turn with blind egoism on other victims, their own children.

This play compares favorably with *La Machine infernale*. While it lacks the poetic dimension of that play, it possesses the chief virtues of good naturalistic theater: psychological depth and insight coupled with a generally liberal and humanitarian view. The energy which animates these characters comes from within them; they are not manipulated; they move in a pattern of realistic complexity; and they are drawn with that knowledgeable sympathy which is perhaps any author's most godlike attribute. I have said that the motive of Cocteau's theater is mainly psychological; but it is chiefly in this play that he succeeds in transmitting the sense of the psyche in situation, involved, committed, acting and acted upon. Cocteau's other plays take place largely in some region beyond the human scene where they enact a psychological problem. *Les Parents terribles* is not the world of problems; it is the world; and we must at least partially agree with M. Lannes. It is one of the peaks of Cocteau's achievement.

Yet the idiom is not, finally, his own. In *Les Parents terribles,* Cocteau has written a fine play in the tradition of Ibsen. But in renouncing the world of myth and poetry where he situates his earlier works he has diminished himself. The public breathed a sigh of relief at *Les Parents terribles;* at last Cocteau had written a play that was accessible, that could be easily situated in the tradition. He was to write two more, each inferior to the preceding, before reasserting his art in its full richness and complexity.

The paradox of
the actor

EVEN MORE THAN *Les Parents, Les Monstres sacrés,* PRODUCED in 1940, is a vehicle play. It was written expressly for Yvonne de Bray, who played the role of a great actress much like herself. Cocteau tells us in his notes to the play that it was written to be acted, that he had his actors in mind, and that this dominated any literary preoccupation.

Besides the wish to provide Yvonne de Bray with a vehicle, he expresses two other intentions for the play. The first is to set down the portrait of a certain artistic type: "This play . . . must give the idea of a Prima Donna, a 'Sacred Monster,' like

Réjane or Sarah Bernhardt." Then he adds, as his ultimate intention: "The goal to attain being to free the audience from a war hypnosis, it is important to make the audience believe that it is in a normal theater, in normal times. It is only after the show that they will be able to say: 'But, as a matter of fact, at what period does all this take place?' If the author and his actors succeed, without forgetting the designer, the trick is pulled off." Cocteau, in the best style of the boulevard author, is setting as his goal the attempt to distract the public.

For the moment, however, let us ignore these aspects of the play, that is, the play as vehicle, the play as "case history," the play as boulevard comedy. The chief interest of *Les Monstres sacrés,* like that of the other minor plays, lies in the insight which it provides into the larger issues of Cocteau's work as a whole. Though imperfect, *Les Monstres sacrés* lends itself to the discussion of a central problem in dramatic art, that is, the problem of the actor. And, since we have seen that for Cocteau the "minor beauty" of the performer is often a symbol or representation of poetry, we may be able to gain more insight from this play than would at first appear likely. A play about actors, it is also a play about art.

The problem of the actor has been a central one in French dramatic criticism ever since it was so neatly formulated by Diderot in his *Paradoxe sur le comédien* (1773). The question at issue was whether or not the actor actually felt the emotions that he portrayed. Rousseau, in his *Lettre à M. D'Alembert sur les spectacles* (1758), had maintained that art deformed the personality. Diderot took the opposite view. For him, the great actor was the critic of his own emotions. He must have "a great deal of judgment" and be "a cold and calm spectator." His job is to "transmit so scrupulously the exterior signs of an emotion that you are deceived." He decrees that "the surest means of acting badly, insignificantly, is to have to act one's own character." He gives an excellent description of esthetic distance and says that art can exist only when the original emotion has been subdued. Hence Rousseau and Diderot represent fairly accurately the two currents of thought on this issue.

For Rousseau, the Romantic, the actor *is* his role. Art and illusion are not possible without the fusion of the artist's personality with the part he is attempting to communicate to the audience. Most actors hold to this point of view, which leads to Stanislavsky and the modern naturalistic school of acting in which the esthetic of identification (between actor and role) is observed.

Diderot, the critical intelligence, represents the other current. It is one which has fewer partisans today, but among them are Bertolt Brecht and Jean-Paul Sartre. Eric Bentley says: "Brecht's criticism of the Stanislavsky system is by this time well known . . . Brecht has asked that the fact of disguise, the dual nature of performance—half actor, half role—be always perceptible. The actor stands back from the role and looks at it; the audience stands back from the actor and looks at him." [1] In Sartre's adaptation of Dumas' *Kean,* the central problem has been radically changed from the original Romantic version. In Dumas' play, the man, Kean, is less real than the actor. The man is his roles. In Sartre's adaptation, the actor knows the play for the lie it is. There is no Romantic identification with the role. Kean says: "One acts in order to lie, to lie to oneself, to be that which one cannot be."

Brecht and Sartre are playwrights of ideas. The play is not so much a vehicle for emotions, for a sense of life, for an imitation of action, as it is a polemical device. The actor serves this polemical function by refusing to be lost in the illusory world of the play. His esthetic distance, always carefully maintained, is a way of reminding the audience that the ideas which are being exposed are valid in reality as well as in the theater.

But Sartre, it will be noted, formulates his attack on art in a work of art. Hence he seems to deny the possibility of identification less than he questions the nature of the two realities involved. It is, of course, Pirandello who makes this question the central theme of his plays.

Cocteau too poses his question about the meaning of the actor's art within a work of art. The outer envelope of *Les Monstres sacrés* is the naturalism of boulevard comedy. But even the world of naturalism is the world of art, and a vast gulf separates the essay or the memoir from the most naturalistic play. These are actors acting a play about acting. So there can be no final denial of art. Art is a mode of the truth, a mode of reality. What we must expect from Cocteau is that he, like Pirandello, will define the reality of art in relationship to other kinds of reality.

The action of the play is as follows: Esther, a great actress, one of the "Sacred Monsters," directs her own theater, much like the late Sarah Bernhardt. She is a kind of high priestess. Her art, like that of Orphée, partakes of the sacred. Indeed, in Act I, scene 3, she says: "The theater is a sort of convent. We serve a god. We repeat the same prayers. We never go to the theater. During the day we do not go out. . . . I add that there are candles, flowers and incense. And that, in all the theaters of the world, the staircases in the wings are like the staircases of prisons." Hence we must take the expression "Sacred Monster" in its most literal sense. Her art harks back to its liturgical origins. And in her uniqueness, her purity, the complete control of voice, body and emotions, Esther is so different from other men and women as to seem a "monster" to them. Esther, in other words, is the priest-poet figure whom we have found to be the heroic archetype in the works of Cocteau. Esther, it should also be observed, is acting in a play called *La Curée* (which might be translated *The Quarry* or *The Hunt*) and in the final scene receives "a deluge of insults." Like the poet-hero, she is persecuted and misunderstood.

Esther's husband, Florent, is a member of the Comédie-Française. The play opens in Esther's dressing room where she receives a visit from an aspiring young actress, Liane, who has seen her performance and been overcome with admiration: ". . . when I saw you . . . I realized that the theater was something—religious." Liane, who is a *pensionnaire* or apprentice actress at the Comédie, tells Esther that Florent is unfaithful to her and that she, Liane, is his mistress.

Esther then accuses Florent of having mixed art and life, of having let something of the role he is playing—Nero in Racine's

Britannicus—infiltrate into his real life as her husband. And she immediately generalizes the theme: "Beware of the theatrical in life. A great actor does his job on the boards. A bad actor acts in life. Do you know who is the worst actor of all? It is the leader who, in order to play a role and be the world's star, doesn't hesitate to cause the death of millions of men. The greatness of the theater is that its corpses get up at the end. But the victims of life's theater don't get up at the end of the play. Do you consider me a great actress? God preserve me from being one at home. And my happiness is dead because I have just learned that Florent does not reserve his acting exclusively for the stage." In other words, she accuses him of the very thing which, for Rousseau, made the actor's vocation immoral: His own personality is absorbed and destroyed by the role he plays.

When Florent appears, however, and denies Liane's assertion that she is his mistress, the young actress breaks down: "A lie. A dirty lie. Listen to me, Madame. I was dying to know you, to share your life, to play a role in it. I made up the whole story. After the show, you made me wild. I had to exult, to act, to burst. I have a very mediocre life of friends and cocktails. I didn't suspect that there were lives like yours— In the theater, I almost never act and I act in failures. I wanted to play a great part, imitate you, astonish you in return." (Act I, scene 6)

Liane suffers by—and also symbolizes—the Romantic conception of the actor which leads to what Cocteau calls "mythomania," the confusion of art and reality. He had written about a mythomaniac in his novel *Thomas l'imposteur,* and the character also crops up in other plays: Margot in *La Machine à écrire* and Lothar in *Bacchus*. The latter kills his hero, Hans, in order that the purity of his myth may not be spoiled. These young men and women try to take a short-cut to fame or happiness. If they themselves cannot be great, they attach themselves to a great idol, some "Sacred Monster." As Esther says to Liane, "Still another girl who loves actresses and not the theater."

Cocteau as a young man was himself a mythomaniac; his avid pursuit of celebrities was a secret attempt to share in their glory. And later he became the mythical source of power to which other young people aspired. Cocteau's countless prefaces to mediocre first editions are his failures, just as Jean Marais is his chief success in the transformation of a young unknown into a national myth or Sacred Monster.

In *La Difficulté d'être* and also in his more recent journal *Maalesh* (1949), Cocteau speaks of the danger of these mythomaniacs. His long enmity with Gide was caused by just such a person: "In order to make himself interesting, to play a role, the idle young man takes part in the stories that he invents. Little by little, doubt infiltrates. The fuse burns, flames, and friendship explodes. Thus moral miles separate men whom five minutes contact would reconcile. Victims of mythomaniacs, we took years to come together and rediscover our former tenderness." [2]

Esther's treatment of Liane, the mythomaniac, is similar to Cocteau's treatment of his mythomaniacs. Act I ends with Esther's decision to take Liane into her home and guide the young actress's career. Note too that Cocteau frequently tries to justify Esther's behavior by having her express a sentiment which he has many times expressed himself. She says in Act II: "I don't know how to hate . . . I don't understand hate. I am incapable of it." (scene 9) Esther is further said to have a "fury to love," and she is accused of having "not the shadow of moral sense." That is to say, she is above the moral categories of normal men and women. She proudly states: ". . . the cleanliness of others would be dirtiness for me." (scene 2) In the first act, Cocteau tells us, Esther embodies a kind of "lucid stupor." All of these details point to her identification with the typical artist-hero.

In Act II, after having literally forced Florent and Liane together, Esther leaves her home. In this act, in which the characters frequently accuse each other of being theatrical and of allowing the theater to deform their lives, the intensity of the drama is heightened by the fact that Florent and Liane are getting ready to leave for a radio broadcast. The radio broadcast cuts short their explanations; there is not time to live life because Florent and Liane must be off to live in the theater. Significantly, they are going to recite Musset's "Nuit d'Octobre." Although we do not actually hear the poem in the play, its general theme (Musset's final liberation from Georges Sand) is familiar to the French public. Florent, as the poet, will proclaim:

C'est une femme à qui je fus soumis
Comme le serf l'est à son maître.

Joug détesté! c'est par là que mon cœur
  Perdit sa force et sa jeunesse. *

After they have gone, Esther says to her friend, Charlotte: "The theater is a frightful world."

Act III begins with a radio interview in Esther's home, where Florent now lives with Liane. The scene is not merely a comic satire on the modern pseudo-theater of the radio. It is a representation of the invasion of the theater in life. Florent, who clings to an older conception of art, refuses to be interviewed. Only Liane, the mythomaniac, takes advantage of the radio to announce falsely that she and Florent are going to be married and that they will honeymoon in Hollywood. She is attempting to use the theatrical, that is, the radio, to influence life, to exert pressure on Florent through public opinion, so that her dreams may be realized.

But Florent hates machines and the machine-dominated radio and cinema. He believes in the slowly acquired art of the classic actor as opposed to the overnight success of the movie star, based on publicity, and profiting by the mythomanic appetites of the masses. When Esther returns to their home on a visit and tells him that she is in love (with someone else he infers, but the audience knows that it is with him), Florent's jealousy is awakened. Both admit finally that they love each other. Liane is sent off to Hollywood by herself. Note that this is a theatrical

---

* I was subject to a woman
    Like a vassal to his master.
  Hateful bondage! thus my heart
    Lost its force and its youth.

device. Esther wins back Florent's love by resorting to a scene that she has probably played many times before.

The author notes as the play comes to an end: "The hysterical laughter of Esther and Florent drowns everything out. It is the relaxation of a theatrical farce after five months of tragic tension." They act as if the tragedy they have lived through were a farce. But what was it? What was the reality and what the illusion? Does the play imply any clear distinction between the emotions which an actor feels in and out of his roles?

The life in art, according to Cocteau, takes many forms. These forms are all represented in the play; the problem is to establish the relationship among them. If we assume for a moment that art and life are truly separate systems, then the play would seem to tell us that the confusion of art and reality is bad, that all of the characters are guilty of it at one time or another, but that Liane is most guilty and Esther least. This is the assumption of Diderot, and many parallels between Cocteau's text and the *Paradoxe sur le comédien* suggest a direct influence.

Liane, for whom Cocteau feels great sympathy, tries to impose her own fantasies, her own dream of art, upon life. Florent and Esther, for whom art is not a dream but an acquired discipline, are able to make the distinction most of the time. Florent says that he considers the theater a means of "désintoxication." When he is on the stage, he "clears himself of all these impure miasmas," that is, the fantasies of crime, dishonesty and infidelity which are potentially in all of us. The comic Charlotte

de Cauville, although the most theatrical in her external behavior, is the least victim of the theatrical in life. She loves her
mother, she pinches the penny and in general shows a laudable
tough-mindedness not apparent in the other characters.

In this view, the play would simply be a lesson pointing out
the dangers of mythomania. The naturalistic envelope would be
appropriate to the basic rationality of such a view; for naturalism attempts to portray the world as it looks to the eye of common sense. And the view that art and reality should not be
mixed would seem to be the product of a common sense judgment. Here we have an adequate justification of the boulevard
formula with its mass appeal. The play espouses a common
sense point of view and presents it as moral lesson to the public.

The difficulties of such an interpretation are twofold. First
of all, the judgment against art is highly conditioned by the
fact that it occurs in a work of art. Of course, art can refer outside of itself to life. This is the position of Brecht and Sartre. It
is also Cocteau's, in some measure, although he would not go
so far as to demand non-naturalistic acting. Indeed, his chosen
genre here is one which (contrary to the strictures of Brecht)
makes naturalism the normal vehicle for the moral thesis. The
fact that the truth about life is presented as an imaginary action,
in the context of a work of art, implies a much higher degree of
mixing than our hypothesis about the separateness of art and
life would allow.

The second flaw in this hypothesis is apparent when we consider the character of Esther. She is not merely a woman who
learns a lesson, not even merely a great actress. She is something

more, namely the artist-hero who returns eternally as myth and prototype in all of Cocteau's works. The clues to her character are those lyrical outbursts which seem to surge up involuntarily, in spite of Cocteau and in spite of herself. She has taken her destiny into her own hands and develops according to a logic which the play does not posit. If we recall for a moment Cocteau's other play in which the artist-as-hero is treated overtly, *Orphée,* we may see what Esther is trying to tell us. Her message contradicts the play's other meaning. It is that art is the completion, the realization of life; that art is a greater truth than life. Although this view does not predominate in the play, it may be felt throughout, for instance in the sympathetic portrayal of Liane. It is like Cocteau's bad conscience, the admission of his final inability to commit himself to the naturalistic form and vision of reality.

In this play, as in every other play of Cocteau's, there is a fundamental duality. Two visions are sustained, like the two meanings of metaphor, like the balance of the acrobat who attempts to reconcile contrary forces. The play is an equation; it remains to be seen whether or not there is a solution.

This play is moderately successful, I think, in its own terms, within the limits of its formula. But, at the same time, it raises problems which go beyond the formula and are not solved. Cocteau does not want to solve the "dramatic equation." The happy ending is the triumph neither of art nor of life. It is only a temporary adjournment of the paradox—as in Diderot's dialogue which ends when one of the speakers says: "But it's getting late. Let's go have dinner." The paradox is even clearer if we put *Orphée* and *Les Monstres sacrés* face to face. These two plays about art arrive at different and contradictory conclusions. The truth, as Cocteau sees it, is in both of them. Ultimately, there is no solution to the paradox: The dramatic equation is merely a form of the balance and/or ambiguity which is the keynote of Cocteau's work. It is another facet of his mystery.

Studies in
mythomania

"He fell. He became deaf, blind. 'A bullet,' he said. 'I'm done for if I don't pretend to be dead.'

"But in him, fiction and reality were one and the same. Guillaume Thomas was dead."

Thomas l'imposteur

IT SEEMS CLEAR THAT COCTEAU'S MESSAGE IS NOT EASILY ADAPTED to the naturalistic form. He thinks in terms of the dramatic image, the high emotion of myth or the broad adventures of a legendary hero whose distance from the everyday world makes him a fitting vehicle for Cocteau's obscure communications and hermetic poetry. *Les Parents terribles* is an exception which nothing in Cocteau's previous works could have led us to expect. And it is in no way equaled by his subsequent plays in this idiom, *Les Monstres sacrés* and *La Machine à écrire*.

La Machine à écrire, Cocteau's third naturalistic play, was produced in April 1941 at the Théâtre Hébertot. Cocteau says in his preface to this play that it cost him more effort than any other he had written. It was rewritten twelve times in an effort to solve the plot. And even then, Cocteau confesses, the play is ruined by a bad ending: "*La Machine à écrire* is a disaster. Already, when I felt ready to write it, another inspiration possessed me and dictated *La Fin du Potomak*. I wanted to get back to it. I took dictation badly. After the first act I went on only out of stubbornness. Once it was written, I forced myself to rewrite it. Finally I listened to suggestions and ruined the ending. That play is an example to me. I will never be my own master. I am made for obedience." He means, that is, that he can write only when obeying some kind of inspiration. But inspiration is not so much, as Cocteau seems to suggest here, a matter of time and place. The difficulties that Cocteau encountered in writing *La Machine à écrire* indicate, not so much that the time to write it had passed, but rather that he was not working in his own medium.

Other difficulties beset Cocteau when the play was produced. Immediately after the dress rehearsal, it was banned, and Cocteau was plunged into new disputes with the authorities. Cocteau's work was branded as decadent and tainted with Judaism. This was the signal for the beginning of those attacks against Cocteau and Jean Marais which reached their climax with the revival of *Les Parents terribles*.

Cocteau first thought of writing such a play while at Tulle, an industrial town 420 kilometers southwest of Paris. Tulle was the scene of a famous case involving anonymous letters, and it is just such a situation that we find in the play. The dull provincial town in which the play takes place is terrorized by an almost diabolical writer of anonymous letters who signs himself "La Machine à écrire"—"The Typewriter." Fred, a detective, is incognito at the home of his friend Didier. He has been detailed to bring the criminal to justice. The action of the play is, ostensibly, the search for the culprit. But Cocteau calls his play a "false detective plot." The real story involves the working out of the relationships of Didier's twin sons, Pascal and Maxime, their adopted sister, Margot, and Solange, a friend of the family. It is practically impossible to reduce the conflict of character to meaningful terms. There are a lot of emotional fireworks, violent arguments between the young people, even a false epileptic fit; but without sufficient motivation in plot.

Maxime is an *enfant terrible.* He has just been discharged from prison, but his family does not know his whereabouts. Subsequently, they learn that he has been living in the château of Solange and that she has become his mistress. Margot, who is engaged to marry Pascal, is really in love with Maxime and is jealous of Solange. Pascal, in turn, is jealous of his brother. Solange is trying to find happiness in the love of Maxime, who is young enough to be her son. Didier plays no appreciable role; Fred is a kind of detective philosopher, mildly apologetic for belonging to the police. He has a fundamental sympathy with criminals, and especially with the "Machine à écrire," who represents a kind of avenging power, bringing into the light the secret greed, cruelty and oppression which Cocteau (who had probably read too much Mauriac) finds lurking in the hearts of provincial Frenchmen. "With *La Machine à écrire,* a false detective plot lets me depict the terrible feudal provinces as they were before the debacle, where, amid vice and hypocrisy, some do a very poor job of protecting themselves, while others (Romanesque youth) are induced to become mythomaniacs."

Following the boulevard formula, each act works up to a surprise. In Act I, Margot confesses that she is the author of the letters. In Act II, Maxime makes the same confession; when no one believes him, he throws a fit. In Act III, Solange is unmasked as the true culprit. Margot leads Maxime back to his family. Fred tries to persuade Solange to let a mentally disturbed girl, the post-mistress, who has confessed to being the "Machine à écrire," take the rap for her. Fred, who is certainly very sentimental for a policeman, even offers to marry Solange. But she refuses, tricks him into permitting her to leave the room by herself, and takes her life.

The play is not what Cocteau says it is, that is, a picture of provincial life. The atmosphere which Cocteau wishes to create—and which emerges so successfully in Mauriac's novels or in *Le Corbeau,* Henri-Georges Clouzot's film on the same subject—is suggested in the most perfunctory way by exposition. There are none of the typical provincial character types. The characters are Cocteau's own: Margot and Maxime, his beloved *enfants terribles,* Solange, the beautiful and neurotic middle-aged woman. Like their prototypes in Cocteau's other plays, these characters are in rebellion. They rebel against the narrowness of provincial life. But we do not see this provincial life dramatized as a concrete threat to happiness. We are merely told about it. This conflict, which is really the central conflict of the play, is expressed by Solange in her confession in Act III, scene 8: "I hated the whole city. All this false happiness, false piety, false luxury, this hypocritical bourgeoisie, so selfish and stingy and irreproachable. I wanted to stir up that mud, attack, unmask. It made me dizzy! Without realizing it, I chose the dirtiest, the vilest weapon: the typewriter." Margot and Maxime confess to Solange's crime because they share her feelings of hatred and rebellion. This hostility to society is similar to the hostility and feelings of persecution that we have seen in practically all of Cocteau's plays.

In *La Machine à écrire* Cocteau presents his main characters—Margot, Maxime and Solange—in an inconclusive way. To begin with, the first two are not especially attractive. Margot has a bad temper, and Maxime's behavior is pathological. They do not win our sympathy. Solange does, even though it is difficult to accept her taking Maxime as her lover. But there is absolutely no preparation for the final revelation of her guilt. We might have been prepared for it if Cocteau had dramatized, had presented before our eyes, the provincial cruelties which are supposed to be the motive for her crime. But there is no real sense of provincial life. And Solange is provided neither with a motive nor with the kind of latent criminality which would make her deed plausible.

It is possible to use a detective story as the vehicle of a deeper truth. But it is necessary, first of all, to accept the detective story convention, to believe in it and develop it with rigorous logic. The implausibility of Cocteau's plot and the lack of definition in his detective, Fred, are not merely imperfections which we can overlook while enjoying the play on another level, say, as *drame bourgeois* in the style of *Les Parents terribles*. Plot cannot be a mere pretext. It must be the metaphor of the play's meaning. The collapse of the plot prevents us from believing in the characters at all. Cocteau was not sure of what he wanted to say in the play, and he was not sure of the form in which he wanted to say it. The persecution theme is not sufficiently forceful, and the detective convention is not fully carried out. The apparent range of Cocteau's art is illusory. He is a writer with only a few themes and a few manners; in writing this play he made the mistake of believing the legend which portrays him as a Jack-of-all-trades.

In 1946 Cocteau offered his *Aigle à deux têtes* to the Parisian public. This play forms a group with *Les Parents terribles, Les Monstres sacrés* and *La Machine à écrire*. The attempt to work within a conventional genre and the absence of the mythological and the marvelous are typical of these plays of Cocteau's later period. *L'Aigle,* unlike the other plays of this group, is not in the naturalistic convention. It is a kind of Romantic melodrama, like Victor Hugo's *Ruy Blas,* of which Cocteau produced a film version in 1947. It is, above all, in terms of theme that *L'Aigle* most resembles the three naturalistic plays. The young queen of *L'Aigle* carries her mythomania further than any other character we have seen so far. In fact, the choice of the melodramatic convention serves precisely this purpose. The sweeping action, verging on the implausible, the passionate, lyrical and extravagant in character and speech, are all justified by the tradition of melodrama. Thus theme and convention authorize each other.

The sweeping action and the exaggerated sentiment are the essence of melodrama. Yet the action and the sentiment of melodrama lack that context of truth which gives the theater its ultimate transcendence, that is, its link with reality, with the world as we know it. It is, in a sense, Cocteau's early fascination with "spectacle" that is felt here. And certainly the melodrama is par excellence the genre of spectacle.

French melodrama, born on the famous "Boulevard du Crime," combined the historical setting derived from the historical dramas of Schiller with the baroque fantasy of the eighteenth century novelists Monk Lewis and Ann Radcliffe. These elaborately machined spectacles, full of intrigue, crime and passion, influenced the Romantic drama of Dumas père and Victor Hugo. Eugène Scribe worked in the same atmosphere of pure suspense which is the property of melodrama.

This seems to be the convention which Cocteau wants us to assume in reading his play. And most of the basic elements of melodrama are present herein.

Like *Bacchus, L'Aigle à deux têtes* is set in a Germanic country split by unrest and rebellion. This approximates the traditional historical setting of the melodrama. The play opens with a storm; there is much listening at doors, shooting of pistols; the baroque atmosphere is enhanced by Tony, a deaf-mute dwarf who is the Queen's servant; there is, finally, the double "suicide" of Stanislas and the Queen. The melodramatic convention calls for these atmospheric devices and for broad characterizations as well.

L'Aigle is the story of an imaginative Queen who has lost all interest in life, plays at life in order to distract herself and, it would seem, to torment her two attendants, Félix de Willenstein and Edith de Berg. The Queen is the poet symbol which we find in every Cocteau play. Significantly enough, her activity is purely gratuitous, like the pure poetic act. Hers is a life of gesture, activity without content. She goes from château to château as the mood strikes her. She engages in target practice in her library, rides on horseback, and so on.

But the Queen finally falls in love with a real poet. His name is Stanislas, and the Queen has first heard of him as the author of a poem attacking her. The poem was signed "Azraël," and it will be recalled that this is the name given to the angel of death who appears in *Orphée*. So Stanislas— played by Jean Marais who has created most of Cocteau's angels on stage or screen—is an angel, a lover and somehow an angel of death. There is a confluence here of Cocteau's favorite symbols.

The veiled Queen appears as the play opens, and as the storm mounts, she sits down by herself at a table set for two. It is the anniversary of her wedding night, which was also the night on which the King died. There is a sound of shooting, and suddenly Stanislas enters the room through the open window. The Queen's guards are at his heels; it is the man-hunt, the *chasse à l'homme,* which we have seen as an important element in *Bacchus.* The Queen is struck by the resemblance between Stanislas and her dead husband. Without further ado, she decides to protect him.

The Queen's intention is to use Stanislas, whom she soon recognizes as a young anarchist-poet who wishes to assassinate her, as the instrument of her death: "What? You ask me who you are? But, dear sir, you are my death. It is *my* death that I save. It is *my* death that I hide. It is *my* death that I warm. It is *my* death that I care for." (Act I, scene 6) Love and death are symbolized by a single person. Stanislas will satisfy the Queen's double wish to love and to die. He is, in a way, the two-headed eagle on the Queen's coat of arms. The eagle is also of course the symbol of the two lovers who cannot live one without the other:

STANISLAS

An eagle with two heads.

THE QUEEN

And if one is cut off, the eagle dies. (Act III, scene 6)

The image of death seems to arise in Cocteau's imagination simultaneously with that of love, and the royal beauty of the actors cannot hide the terror which underlies this identification. The fact that Stanislas and the Queen become lovers seals their death warrant.

Stanislas and the Queen are poets. It is inevitable then that their purity will set them apart from the world of men. So the Queen says in Act II, scene 9: "The beauty of tragedy, its human and superhuman interest, is that it portrays nothing but beings who live above all laws. What were we tonight: An idea confronting an idea. And now what are we? A hunted woman and a hunted man. Equals." She seems to say that to "live above all laws" is inevitably to be "hunted." The poet is hunted down because of his purity. This would seem to be Cocteau's stock theme, the theme which he turns to almost automatically, in obedience to some fatality as mysterious as that which weighs upon his characters. But we need not accept the theme at its face value; we can give it a twist, see it from a slightly different angle. Are the characters actually persecuted by the world? Or does the mere fact of a love commitment inspire them with a feeling of horror that they *explain* as persecution? They cannot bear the reality of involvement, and so they (literally in this play) commit suicide.

For a time, their love gives Stanislas and the Queen a new power, and they attempt to ward off disaster. This attempt to struggle against the "others," to circumvent their destiny, is the dramatic nexus of the play. The Queen's enemies are the Archduchess and the head of the Queen's police, the Count de Foëhn. They are involved in a shadowy intrigue with certain revolutionary forces. Before shifting his allegiance to the Queen, Stanislas was one of these revolutionaries. He had been hired by the Count to kill the Queen.

The ease with which Stanislas changes sides, discovering, in effect, that his desire to kill the Queen had really been a fascination, almost a kind of love for her, indicates the minor importance of the political theme. The characters are not in any sense committed, struggling for a cause. Self-interest seems to be their only motive; and it is hard to assign any motive at all to the Count, who is an empty, puppet-like character, manipulated by the author to the accompaniment of cynical smiles, moustache-twirling and sinister *double-entendre*. This, again, is in the melodramatic formula. But we see in the failure to become really "engaged" what I have called the lack of transcendence. The author would have us accept his play on the level of psychological truth. But a character which lacks one kind of reality tends by this fact to become unreal on all levels.

For a while, Stanislas and the Queen attempt to struggle against the fatal destiny in which they both secretly believe. They repeat a "charm" or spell, a magic formula with which to ward off disaster: "Lord, accept us in the kingdom of your enigmas. Protect our love from the contact with men's eyes. Marry us in heaven." (Act II, scene 10)

Stanislas persuades the Queen to unveil, that is, to give up her life of dream and whimsy and return to practical affairs. He wishes her to take the reins of government. She is preparing to enter her capital triumphantly; plans are made to arrest the Count de Foëhn; but, rather inexplicably, Stanislas poisons himself. He says: "I didn't act out of fear. In a flash, I realized that nothing was possible between us, that I had to set you free and disappear while we were still happy." (Act III, scene 8) The Queen is unable to go on without Stanislas. As he stands dying before her eyes, she provokes and taunts him. Finally, he stabs her. If one of the eagle's heads is cut, the eagle dies.

Stanislas and the Queen crumble like marionettes. They have no power of resistance. They cannot struggle. Perhaps it is because thay have nothing to struggle for. Mythomaniacs, they believe only in themselves. They have the charm of youth, enthusiasm, beauty; and, of course, they benefit by some of the magnificent speeches which Cocteau has given them. Or perhaps their trouble is that they do not even believe in themselves. The Queen cannot believe she is a Queen. Stanislas cannot believe that he is worthy to be her lover. These characters are always in action, but it is a restless action, without meaning or content. They never stop to enjoy the fulfillment of their love. Significantly, the Queen "makes-believe" that she does not love Stanislas in order to provoke him to kill her. And because she has so little reality, he believes the "make-believe." Again he shifts his allegiance. Almost petulantly, he kills her. Neither character has any sense of his own or the other's reality. It is fear, fear of being themselves and choosing a course of action, which kills them. They are their own enemies and their own destroyers.

Les Monstres sacrés, La Machine à écrire and *L'Aigle à deux têtes* represent the two aspects of mythomania. There is, first, the adulation of someone else, the desire, usually on the part of a young person (Liane in *Les Monstres sacrés*), to insinuate himself into the life of his idol, to steal some of that idol's sacred fire. Second, as an almost inevitable corollary, there is lack of belief in Self. This is disguised by irresponsible and extravagant behavior, as in the case of the Queen in the present play. She seizes on love not for its own sake, as an end in itself, but as a prop. She needs her lover's strength in order to be a real queen. But he, alas, is no stronger than she. Because neither has any real strength, both collapse, each having mistakenly depended on the other. It scarcely seems that an eagle is a fitting symbol for these lovers.

We have now examined all except one of Cocteau's major plays. The heroes and heroines of all these plays have certain important traits in common. They are either "angels" or mythomaniacs, that is, young persons who try desperately to establish themselves in the world, often by criminal means, although, by their very nature, they are doomed to failure. They fail because of some inability to accept real commitment, no matter how much they seem to desire it. By skillful manipulation of these characters Cocteau makes their failure significant and creates about them a strange and fascinating world which moves and disturbs us despite its limited dramatic appeal.

Poetry
as charm

IN ALL HIS BIBLIOGRAPHIES, COCTEAU LISTS HIS NOVELS, CRITICISM, plays and other works under the generic title of poetry: *poésie du roman, poésie critique, poésie du théâtre.* There is a kind of generalized poetic character, he would have us believe, which is independent of the form or even the object in which it inheres. Jean Hytier, in his *Les Arts de littérature,* compares the "poetic pleasure," taken in this broad sense, with the "esthetic pleasure" which bears a strict relation to the *form* of the object: "In reality, poetic pleasure is a very general pleasure that is experienced often, not always, in works of art, but just as well elsewhere, and never as a function of an esthetic value." "It [esthetic pleasure] seems to us to be chiefly intellectual, while poetic pleasure is chiefly affective, the latter pleases without art, while the other pleases by art." [1]

Appropriating M. Hytier's distinction to the works of Cocteau, we might look on the poet's development as the forging of a vehicle which raises the crude poetic impulse toward greater and greater esthetic perfection. The esthetic pleasure of Cocteau's early ballets and plays lay chiefly in spectacle and other expressionistic devices. These devices were poetic, but the plays as a whole were not poetry. The purpose of the drama was only to communicate the devices. In the plays of Cocteau's middle period, the characters, action and diction seemed to move in the direction of poetic complexity and expressiveness. So Cocteau's esthetic became a more and more suitable vehicle for poetry. We might say, in M. Hytier's words, that he was learning "a technique of poetization." [2] *Les Chevaliers de la Table Ronde,* which prepares Cocteau's emergence as a dramatic poet, shows the poetic function of plot, plot as metaphor. But there is no truly poetic drama without verse, that is, poetry of language. In *Renaud et Armide* we find the complete and articulated vehicle of the poetic impulse which runs so strongly through all of Cocteau's works.

Renaud et Armide was first produced in April 1943 at the Comédie-Française, with Marie Bell in the role of Armide and Maurice Escande as Renaud. Two things distinguish *Renaud et Armide* from all of Cocteau's other plays: It is purely and simply a love story, and it is written in verse.

Tasso created the legend of Armida in his *Gerusalemme Liberata*. Armida herself is an invention based, perhaps, on the enchantress Idraote in the romance *Merlin* by the thirteenth century Burgundian poet Robert de Boron. Armida is the daughter of a Siren who lived in the river Euphrates. She is the incarnation of sensual pleasure and the false delights of the spirit bewitched by love. In Tasso, from whom Cocteau takes his plot, the hero Rinaldo lingers on the fabled island of Fortuna with Armida, who is deeply in love with the Christian hero and practices all her spells to hold him. But the captain of the Christian army, Goffredo Buglione, sends for Rinaldo, whose help is needed in battle; and with a solemn goodbye, Rinaldo leaves the despairing Armida. (In Tasso's work they are later reunited, and Armida is converted to Christianity.) The enchanted garden, the nymphs and sensual atmosphere of Tasso provide a verbal and emotional basis for Cocteau's transposition of the legend to the theater. There was already a great deal of inherent "poetry" in the material with which Cocteau began to work.

The action of the play takes place in an enchanted garden. In Act I, scene 1, the knight Olivier whispers to Renaud:

> Sire, parlez plus bas.
> Ce vide est de l'enfer. Ce faux soleil envoûte.
> La lumière regarde et le silence écoute.*

> * Sire, speak more softly.
> This emptiness is hellish. This false sun casts a spell.
> The light watches and the silence listens.

The enchantment of Armide's garden is immediately realized in the poetic imagery: The light watches and the silence listens. In scene 3, Olivier observes,

> Un soleil fixe éclaire un jardin de métal
> Où la plus simple fleur ouvre une bouche étrange.*

In scene 4, in an extraordinary poetic outburst, Renaud cries to his soldiers to come and torture the garden until it reveals the hiding place of Armide:

> Dans ces jardins, soldats, quelque secret se cache.
> Soldats, torturez-les et qu'on le leur arrache.
> Qu'on traîne, s'il le faut, l'arbre par les cheveux!
> A moi, soldats! Brisez, saccagez ce mystère!
> Arbre, fleur, herbe, roc, retournez cette terre. . .
>   Mais torturez-la donc!
> Teignez-vous de ce sol et de sa boue humide,
> Obtenez qu'il vous dise où se cachait Armide. . .
> Que ce jardin avoue en demandant pardon!
>
> Criez, jardins, criez d'une voix hors nature.
> Soldats, mes chers soldats, redoublez la torture,
>   Et, pareils aux rameurs,
> Labourez-moi de fer ces vagues de désordre.
> Et si jamais la terre essayait de vous mordre,
> Tuez! Frappez! Armide, au secours! je me meurs!

* A fixed sun lights a metallic garden
  Where the simplest flower opens a strange mouth.

Je me meurs! Qu'ai-je fait? Qu'est-ce que je décide?
Je sens que ce jardin c'est elle, c'est Armide.
   Un enchanteur puissant,
A, jadis, en jardin, transformé la princesse.
Armide, suis-je ici pour que le charme cesse?
Et moi qui commandais de verser votre sang!

Je comprends qu'un jardin puisse avoir cet empire.
Mais que disais-je encore? Hé quoi, le mal est pire!
   Un désespoir soudain
Me montre que mes bras n'étreignent que du vide.
Je croyais adorer dans le jardin d'Armide,
Et j'y cherchais Armide et j'aimais un jardin.*

---

* In these gardens, soldiers, a secret is hiding.
  Soldiers, torture them and tear it from them.
  Drag, if you must, the tree by its hair!
  Here, soldiers! Break, pillage this mystery!
  Tree, flower, grass, rock, plow up that earth.
    But torture it then!

  Stain yourself with this soil and its damp mud,
  Make it tell you where Armide was hiding,
  And let this garden confess and beg my pardon!

  Cry out, gardens, cry out with an unnatural voice.
  Soldiers, dear soldiers, redouble the torture,
    And, like oarsmen,
  Beat with steel these disorderly waves.
  And if ever the earth try to attack you,
  Kill! Strike! Armide, help! I am dying!

  I am dying! What have I done? What shall I decide?
  I feel that this garden is she, is Armide.
    A powerful magician,

The garden, which is the structural metaphor of the play, acquires the attributes of a living being as the action unfolds; indeed, its function in the play is as important as that of either main character. From the garden of the *Roman de la Rose* to T.S. Eliot's rose garden, the garden has been a poetic locale at once suggestive and vague, capable of wide analogizing, and above all, proper to love poetry. *Renaud et Armide* is a play about a particular kind of love, specifically, love as obstructed. This is one of the earliest conceptions of secular love to be found in literature: It is found in the troubadours, kept from their mistresses by social barriers; it is the theme of Dante and Racine; and it returns to poetry with the Romantics, whose love was obstructed not by obstacles exterior to themselves but by their very incapacity to love. Cocteau's play does not present the impediments to love in any concrete substantive way; the enchantment of the garden is an allegorical representation of inner impediments such as are found in the Romantic tradition.

Nature imagery or the garden, which so often appears in

Once upon a time, transformed the princess.
Armide, am I here so that the spell may cease?
And I who was ordering that your blood be spilled!

I understand that a garden might have such a power.
But what was I just saying? Indeed, the evil is greater!
  A sudden despair
Shows me that my arms embrace only emptiness.
I thought I was in love in the garden of Armide,
And I looked for Armide and I loved a garden.

love poetry, is more than a backdrop or décor; it becomes the symbol of the psychological life, of the human heart, which is itself the setting for the experience of love as well as the chief actor in love's drama. The enchanted garden of *Renaud et Armide* is Cocteau's symbolic representation of the attempt to love; the obsessive image-making and incantation found in this play point to the difficulties involved in a love commitment. Indeed, to extend the metaphor, the confining garden walls might well be considered as those unhealthy fears and compulsions which are the chief obstacle to love and which appear, in more concrete forms, in other works of Cocteau.

The dangers of the garden—that is, the constrictive and repressive fantasies of the unconscious—are represented by Armide's fairy consorts, of whom all but Oriane are invisible. Little by little, as the poetic detail accumulates, there is generated an uncomfortable sense of being watched. There is no privacy in this garden, even when the lovers are alone.

The impossibility of a love which is impeded by unconscious fears and inhibitions is perfectly represented in the first act by the anguish of the enchanted lovers as they search for each other in vain. In the first scene, Renaud searches for Armide but does not find her; in scene 2 she appears, but Renaud has been put into a magic sleep; as she disappears, he wakes and begins to search for her again. In scene 4 Renaud attempts in vain to invoke her by the threat of force. In scene 5, Armide speaks, invisible this time, and complains of the torments of love: "Jamais en aucun lieu je ne me trouve à

l'aise . . ."—"Never in any place am I at ease . . .". The long
complaint is formed by a series of antitheses, in the Petrarchian
manner, and is based on the paradox that love is a torment. But
here in this garden, the obstacles to love are not, as in the
Petrarchian tradition, the lady's indifference or remoteness.
They are of a different and less tangible order. This part of
the act is a kind of hide-and-go-seek, a slipping into and
emerging from the enchanted world symbolized by the personified garden. It is in this tense climate that the lovers finally
speak to each other, although Armide remains invisible.

In Act I, scene 5, Renaud and Armide imagine that they
have joined hands. This imagined contact is expressed in a
series of verbal paradoxes: Are they hot or cold? alive or
dead? The interpretation of this joining of the lovers' hands
is given in an image:

ARMIDE

*   *   *

Les veines de ta main conduisent à ton cœur.
Il bat ton cœur.

RENAUD

       Si fort qu'il annonce un malheur.
C'est comme le cheval du malheur qui galope.

ARMIDE

J'y colle mon oreille. Ecoute: une syncope. . .
Il s'arrête. Il repart. Il repart au galop.
Il s'arrête. Il repart.

RENAUD

Il annonce un complot.
Contre nous. Un malheur. Il galope. Il m'éveille.

ARMIDE

Ce n'est pas un malheur qu'il dit à mon oreille.
Renaud, c'est ton amour.

RENAUD

J'ai peur du sang qui court.

ARMIDE

Je veux fuir loin de moi sur ce cheval d'amour! *

* ARMIDE

* * *

The veins of your hand lead to your heart.
Your heart beats.

RENAUD

So strongly that it announces a misfortune.
It is like the galloping horse of unhappiness.

ARMIDE

I fasten my ear there. Listen: a syncope—
It stops. It starts again. It starts to gallop.
It stops. It starts.

RENAUD

It announces a plot
Against us. A misfortune. It gallops. It wakes me.

ARMIDE

It is not a misfortune that my ear hears.
Renaud, it is your love.

RENAUD

I am afraid of this swift blood.

ARMIDE

I want to flee far from myself on this horse of love!

The speed of the heart and of the horse are caught by the short sentences and broken rhythm. From the moment in which their hands first touch there is neither joy nor peace in the love of Renaud and Armide. Their love is symbolized by the "horse of unhappiness," a symbol of terror and flight. Although the setting does not change, the whole play is like a flight through the dense foliage of the imagination into the "safety" of pure poetry.

The paradox of the lovers who touch without touching suggests other quixotic aspects of the neurotic psyche. These lovers do not, or dare not, take what they really want. Hence Renaud desires Armide only to reject her when, in Act II, scene 2, she finally appears to him. He cries:

> Olivier! Olivier! Je suis libre!
> Je vais enfin des murs chercher le talisman.
> Nous pourrons nous sauver de ces jardins. . .*

Love is expressed as a desire for flight—the "cheval d'amour," and the lovers deny the real in favor of the unreal world of fantasy. So Oriane tells Armide: "Renaud adore en vous une énigme." These characters are never comfortable in the presence of emotion; they are always attempting to transmute emotion into language. Cocteau's poetry attempts to produce a kind of emotional liquefaction, that is, to remove the psycho-

---

*   Olivier! Olivier! I am free!
   I can at last look for the talisman of the walls.
   We can escape from these gardens.

logical obstacle to love or to deny the validity of the emotion itself, and hence to change or negate the real world.

The garden of Armide draws its fascination from a strongly implied analogy with the "garden" of the heart. Much of the play's force arises from our ability to make this allegorical connection without being aware of it, to feel it rather than to understand it, just as the unconscious acts only when suppressed.

Renaud can love Armide only in the states of hypnosis (Act I), madness (Act II), or under a magic spell (Act III). So it is that in Act II, scene 3, Armide recites her spell and causes Renaud to lose his reason:

RENAUD

Savez-vous la ballade
Du roi Renaud? Elle aime un pauvre roi malade.
Un roi. . . Vous connaissez Armide? Connaissez-
Vous Armide, Madame? Et le roi? C'est assez
Triste. Connaissez-vous la ballade? Elle est triste.
C'est, paraît-il, un chant qui point encore n'existe.
Connaissez-vous Armide? Il la cherchait en vain.
Connaissez-vous Renaud qui de guerre revint?
Connaissez-vous Renaud qui portait ses entrailles?
Madame, entendez-vous sonner ses funérailles? *

*   Do you know the ballad
Of king Renaud? She loves a poor sick king.
A king—You know Armide? Do you know
Armide, Madame? And the king? It is quite
Sad. Do you know the ballad? It is sad.

Olivier attempts to save Renaud by prayer; there ensues a battle of magic, interrupted by the childlike meanderings of Renaud:

OLIVIER (*bas*)

Roi du ciel. . .

ARMIDE (*à Renaud*)

Dors, Renaud.

OLIVIER (*bas*)

Venez à mon secours. . .

ARMIDE

Je te berce. . .

RENAUD

Connaissez-vous Armide?

ARMIDE

Je te berce. . .

OLIVIER

Saint Georges à cheval qui le dragon transperce,

Saint Denis qui portez votre tête. . .

(*Renaud s'agite.*)

ARMIDE

Qu'as-tu?

Dors, Renaud.

It is, it seems, a song which does not yet exist.
Do you know Armide? He looked for her in vain.
Do you know Renaud who came back from war?
Do you know Renaud who carried his own entrails?
Madame, do you hear his funeral tolling?

OLIVIER

> Saint Michel qui vous êtes battu
> Contre Satan lui-même, empêchez qu'on nous dupe.*

Olivier's prayers seem to reach a higher power than Armide's magic, for Renaud suddenly asks for Armide's ring, the ring which, if she gives it to him, will restore his reason and cause her death. Olivier uses language as a means of transforming

---

* OLIVIER (*softly*)
  King of heaven,

  ARMIDE
  > Sleep, Renaud.

  OLIVIER (*softly*)
  > > Come to my aid.

  ARMIDE
  I rock you.

  RENAUD
  > Do you know Armide?

  ARMIDE
  > > I rock you.

  OLIVIER
  Saint George on horseback who pierces the dragon,
  Saint Denis, you who carry your own head.

  (*Renaud stirs.*)

  ARMIDE
  > > What is the matter?
  Sleep, Renaud.

  OLIVIER
  > Saint Michael who fought
  Against Satan himself, prevent them from tricking us.

reality, of wresting something from it, producing a change by the reiteration of sacred and mysterious words. Throughout this act, Renaud speaks as a madman, reciting an ancient ballad, searching for the truth through the haze of insanity. He is trying to exorcise himself, to free himself from the spell, the enchanted graden.

In Act III, Armide finally gives Renaud the magic ring. His reason is restored, and he is free to return to his army, his wife and kingdom. But the giving of the ring, a very ancient symbol of sexual union, has caused the two of them to fall hopelessly in love. Yet they may not embrace; for one kiss will cause Armide's death. This explicit linking of love and death (just as in *L'Aigle à deux têtes*) is another expression of the fear of emotion and the familiar chaos of normal life.

At last, for a moment, love seems possible. Armide gives the ring to Renaud: *"The shadows scatter. Everything grows calm. The daylight which arises is that of a luminous morning. Sunlight replaces the diffused light. Armide has put aside all her magical attributes. She is kneeling, stage right, her hair loosened, dressed in white. Renaud is on his knees, facing her, on the left."* For a moment Renaud and Armide exist in a pure, untroubled world. It is the pristine world in which the Grail is manifested to the knights of the Round Table or the final scene of *Orphée* when the settings mount up into the sky. Yet it does not last. The enchantment of the ring has not been exhausted. Renaud embraces Armide, and she dies. For all its limpid poetry and powerful lyricism, *Renaud et Armide* leaves us finally in a haunted garden with the last words of a ceaseless enchantment ringing in our ears.

The enchanted garden is the source of most of the play's imagery. It dominates everything, giving organic continuity to the whole play. But the play has other forms of unity. Although it is in three acts, instead of the customary five, it preserves the classical unities of time, place and action. It further resembles a Racinian tragedy in the use of the characters, four in number: Armide and her confidante, Oriane; Renaud and his confidant, Olivier.

Like Racine's *Bérénice,* the play's action is generated by obstructed love. The movement of the play is halting, however. It does not have the ineluctable symmetry of a Racine play. It is as if the characters were alternately waking and falling asleep, finding and losing each other in a ceaseless chase to the rhythm of the four-beat Alexandrine line. The first words of the play are: "Réveillez-vous, Renaud, et reprenez vos armes" —"Awake, Renaud, and take up your weapons." Olivier is the voice of reason, trying to win Renaud from Armide's spells. Several lines later, this Racinian note is struck:

OLIVIER

Se peut-il qu'un roi, qu'un chef vainqueur,
Accepte que sa gloire obéisse à son cœur,

Et, perdant d'un seul coup des triomphes sans nombre,
Se laisse prendre au piège et coure après une ombre? *

The very important difference between Renaud and, say, Racine's Tite is that the latter acts finally on the basis of a reasoned moral judgment. Renaud, on the contrary, is scarcely allowed the use of his reason. From one end of the play to the other, he is the victim of Armide's charms and spells. Armide herself is enchanted; the meaning of the whole play is tied up with this use of magic, a magic which is concretized in the enchanted garden. Very specifically, then, the narrative framework justifies and even necessitates the use of poetry as incantation or exorcism. It is similar to what Paul Valéry has called the use of poetry as a "charm": "The efficacity of the 'charms' was not in the meaning resulting from their terms as much as in their sonorities and in the peculiarities of their form. Even obscurity was sometimes essential to them. . . . Death sometimes submitted to rhythmical conjurations, and the tomb released a specter. Nothing more ancient, nor indeed more *natural* than that belief in the force proper to words, a force that was considered to act much less by its *exchange value* [with an abstract prose equivalent, an idea] than by I know not what resonances that it was thought to create in the substance of beings." [3] With *Renaud et Armide* we return to the world of pure poetry proposed to us by Mallarmé and Valéry.

* Can it be that a king, a triumphant chieftain,
Allows his glory to obey his heart,
And, losing in one instant triumphs without number,
Lets himself be trapped and runs after a shadow?

One aspect of the pure poetry movement appears especially relevant to this section of our study of Cocteau. This is the sense in which poetry was used as an escape from immediate reality, or, to state it even more strongly, the sense in which poetry became an attempt to abolish the physical world. Marcel Raymond in his *De Baudelaire au Surréalisme* finds the main theme of Valéry's poetry in the conflict between reality and the world of pure imagination. In "La Jeune Parque" and "Le Cimetière Marin" "a struggle is joined between two contrary attitudes: the *pure* (absolute) attitude, that of consciousness which withdraws into its isolation, and the opposite attitude, which is impure, of an intelligence which accepts life, change, action, and renounces its dream of perfect integrity to let itself be seduced by things and link up with their metamorphoses." [4] M. Raymond sees Valéry's two greatest and most typical poems as the scene of a struggle; but perhaps it is this very struggle itself—rather than its resolution, which would be impossible— which is the real theme of all pure poetry.

Poets are by nature realists; that is, they believe in the existence of objects. The world acts upon them too strongly for them to deny its existence. The image itself must always be to some extent concrete. It can never be completely emptied of all residue of the particular, the concrete, the real. The attempt to write *pure* poetry is therefore inherently contrary to the very nature of the poetic act. Such an attempt produces an almost intolerable state of tension within the poet, who becomes, in effect, not one being but two. He is first of all the poet, committed to the world of concrete objects, and second, the pure spirit, the idealist philosopher, attempting to sublimate his sense of concrete reality and to find the explanation of the world in a mental construct. Such an effort represents an attempt to break down the "concrete universal" by an impossible retreat into the abstract, the pure, the ideal. It is in this way that we can explain the anguish and the admitted failure of Mallarmé as well as the long silences of Valéry. They had pushed their art to such a stage of purity that the struggle could not continue. If they had gone further, they would no longer have been writing poetry.

Cocteau's conception of poetry as machine is a restatement of some of the ideas of Mallarmé and Valéry. It represents an attempt to empty the images of a poem of their concrete significance in favor of some generalized impression or effect, frequently an effect of purely verbal excitement. Poetry is not considered a form of perception or knowledge of the real world. It becomes the poet's intuition of himself. The poem is directed inward. It represents an intuition of the poet by himself; and it is at the same time a lever by which the poet may "charm" himself into some state of contemplative vision or merely verbal and sensual excitement.

Cocteau clearly indicates such a view of poetry in the following lines: "Of course, he [the poet] consoles himself with the pretext that his work participates in some more solid mystery. But that hope arises from the fact that every man is a night (shelters a night), that the work of the artist will be to bring that night to full daylight, and that this secular night

procures for man, who is so limited, an extension of limitless-
ness which relieves him. Man becomes then like a sleeping
paralytic, dreaming that he walks." [5] Poetry cannot lead us
to knowledge of anything beyond ourselves, beyond the obscurity of our own imaginations. Hence, poetry is not to be
considered a transcendental power. It cannot give knowledge
of the noumenal world and must be limited to purely phenomenal knowledge. The poet's consciousness, which cannot finally
attach itself to any created thing, engages in a ceaseless modula-
tion, that "charm" of which Valéry speaks. Mallarmé defines
poetry as "the Orphic explanation of the Earth, which is the
poet's sole duty and par excellence the literary Game." The
world, that is, is not an object of poetry in its own right. It is
a source of symbols, a pretext to the poet's intuition of his own
imagination.

Like Mallarmé and Valéry, Cocteau is interested in the way
in which poetry orders and equilibrates the inner world. The
circus tight-rope walker is a frequent symbol in his poetry and
essays. The poet is like an acrobat suspended over an abyss
which is really his own soul; the precarious power of his art
saves him from the constant threat of "death": "Over the
emptiness, not to break one's neck requires efforts which became my only politics." [6] It is not a literal death that Cocteau
fears. Death is the symbol of some mysterious, unnamed psychic
disaster which might be madness, or might be, on the other
hand, no more than the punishment which a strict mother
metes out to her bad boy. The psychic problems of Renaud

and Armide, indeed, of almost all Cocteau's characters, are solved by a verbal flight; in this fashion they hold their fears—of which death is only the symbol—in equilibrium.

Cocteau's whole theory of style as the elegant balance of opposites grows out of this struggle with death. The mystery of language, of the metaphor, is the mystery of man; our freedom is to turn within this narrow circle which our imagination describes. There is a certain peace or at least an abatement of fear in the contemplation of our mystery. But this peace is always threatened. Below the vibrating wire, the crowd is always waiting breathlessly for the acrobat to fall.

Mallarmé and Valéry were writers of prose essays and lyric poetry. Their flight towards the ideal was consistent with the genres in which they worked. But there is an obvious paradox in the application of this theory to dramatic poetry. A play requires real people, passion and conflict. The dramatic poet's aim is not to abolish these but to make them more real. Yet Cocteau is attempting to perform such an act of negation. The play's magic is an attempt to transform and change, if not abolish, the physical and moral world in which the characters exist. Dramatic poetry explores an experience through metaphorical language. The words always lead back into the experience. But in Cocteau, the poetry leads away from the experience. It tends to nullify the experience, make it abstract and verbal.

This is Cocteau's problem; and it is the problem of his characters as well. They seem to ask: How can I act significantly in the world of beings, events and actions when I mistrust this world and when I find at hand an admirable device—pure poetry—for turning my back on all forms of commitment? We have seen that Cocteau's heroes are most dramatically successful when they are placed in a persecution situation. The reason is obvious: Only some kind of pressure from *outside* can justify their compulsion to flight, although this is merely an objectification of an *inner* pressure to which the character is blind and which the author does not choose to render into action. The use which the typical Cocteau hero or heroine makes of lyricism is related to the pressure under which he finds himself and from which he is trying to get free. He escapes into language, into the continuity of a " charm" which is uncommitted to any single thing.

Such a flight from action is undramatic. And yet these characters possess another quality which makes them stageworthy and saves Cocteau's theater from the danger of a static and unrelated lyricism. It is their theatricality—a theatricality which arises from an obscure presentiment of their problem and an elaborate attempt to circumvent it. They are always on the verge of commitment, feigning commitment, appropriating its language and its poses. They seem very often to be on the point of taking a stand in regard to politics or theology, but they are really doing no such thing; it is enough that they pretend. The pretense is a satisfactory substitute for the real thing. Mythomania is a substitute for real achievement. The various forms of angelism are all parodies of corresponding virtues. By a parody the character satisfies his imagination while postponing the fatal decision, until, at last—in accordance with his secret desire—destiny traps and destroys him. Their theatricality, that is, their poses and pretenses, are their real heroism; for they know that their destruction is close and do nothing about it. They prefer to act out fanciful parodies of roles they will never play; and somehow their pretense gives them courage to face their destruction. It is a kind of reverse heroism that arises from turning one's back on danger rather than facing it. But it is heroism enough to sustain the power and authenticity of Cocteau's dramatic fictions.

Here we have the final explanation of Cocteau's interventions in the plays, his breaking of the dramatic illusion. It is as if he were telling us that the actors are not real and that behind the parody of their art lies something infinitely more touching and more profound. But what that is, neither they—nor he—can tell us.

SINCE WORLD WAR II METAPHYSICS HAS ACQUIRED A NEW PLACE in a literature which, although anchored in the world of the concrete, aspires to the universal and the general. The new emphasis on rational inquiry has, as its corollary, the demand for involvement, for rational participation in the cultural community. Such a literature is strongly opposed to the expressionism of which Cocteau is perhaps the most eminent representative in our time.

The new literature of involvement, however, was not achieved without the struggle of an age of transition, an age in which the limitations of pure art and pure expression first appeared as obstacles to be overcome. This transition is evident in Cocteau, in the constriction and anguish of his plays, in his constant self-interrogation as well as his continual experiments with form. The negative aspects of Cocteau's work—the ambiguity of his moral vision, the calculated hesitations of his characters, the uncommitted balance of his metaphors—represent a transitional phase in the great tradition of negative or alienated literature which comes to us from the Romantics.

Negation, of course, has many meanings. We might in general distinguish two main types of negation: of the Self and of the world. The oldest form of the first type is the emptying of Self, the surrendering of the will to which the mystics exhort us. This is related to the secular conception which we find in Wordsworth and Keats and which the latter called Negative Capability, a concept in turn somewhat similar to Gide's *disponibilité,* that is, a passive receptiveness to experience, based on a suspension of the will. On the cognitive rather than the affective side, there is the Hegelian conception of negation as the foundation of knowledge. Lionel Trilling in his recent book *The Opposing Self* describes that negation of Self (he considers it the true path of self-discovery) which arises from acceptance of life as conditioned, that is, the negativity of "pure spirit" which allows itself to be limited by the biological, social and moral orders.

Sartre gives us another fertile conception of alienation in his studies of Baudelaire and Genet, both of whom he sees as alienated from their true Selves. They must perform a continual act of negation in order to continue to see the factitious social images which they have chosen in preference to their own reality. Their literary works are the myth of their alienation. The work and the writer mutually symbolize each other. Both point to a concealed negation. But there are also forms of negation of the world by the will which turns back upon itself in the effort to renew and revitalize itself or to shift its object. Here we must list such a Nietzschean figure as Rimbaud. And, for his counterpart on the cognitive side, Mallarmé, in whom we find the negation of the meanings of words in pursuit of their associative functions.

This very schematic outline may perhaps serve to give precedent and prestige to the negativity of Cocteau's art. There is alienation from society here, although not to the degree found in Genet and Baudelaire. Although there is a persistent avoidance of rational plots, comparable to Mallarmé's syntactical disarticulation, Cocteau has not created a metaphysic of overtones and associations in Mallarmé's systematic fashion. In Cocteau, the will never achieves that stasis which seems to characterize Negative Capability in Mr. Trilling's sense. His characters achieve neither the *dénoûment* nor the *disponibilité* of Gide. There is, on the contrary, a persistent effort to unleash the will. The will swings back and forth, alternately negating itself and the world, struggling against fierce psychological inhibitions. The will is struggling, precisely, against fear. Cocteau does not choose his negativity; he struggles against it, against all its forms which are, finally, reducible to the one. Fear is the protean antagonist of all his plays.

In this struggle we sense the real tragic stature of Cocteau's art. We might call it the tragedy of negation or the tragedy of impotent will. In Cocteau, will has not been discovered, created, achieved—and this would seem to be the true precondition for the negation of will; it is in process. We see in Cocteau the end result of a long tradition of negation. The will has not been able to make that creative return, out of itself, into the world. The props have been cut away. The classical Cartesian world of essences no longer exists to solicit the will to action. How, indeed, does the will make that necessary return which is choice, affirmation, creation? Cocteau has not shown us that. He has shown us the process, the effort, the struggle, to affirm values where none really exist. In his case the effort is further hampered by enormous psychological barriers; the will has become lost in an enchanted garden of its own making; it cannot get back to the world. But the psychological obstacles are themselves the result, the by-product, of the breakdown of values which we can attribute, in some degree, to the prophets of negation. Cocteau's tragedy of impotent will is the testimony of an age.

Cocteau has outlived his own frivolity, and we begin to see that it was frivolity with a meaning. There is a presentiment of the new order of things which the second world war made a necessity; and a last-ditch struggle to give the old values new meaning. Art is often prophetic, but it is just as often retrospective. It attempts to give new life to fading values and conventions in the face of change; perhaps it is only at such a moment, when the values of a preceding generation have passed into history, that they can be expressed most perfectly in a work of art. It is then that they become myths and achieve their full stature and influence.

This is not merely an appeal to our nostalgia for the past. It is above all a criticism and a creation of the past in which the true meaning of events can finally be made clear. The works of Cocteau are of this nature. In his unflinching perseverance to search, to struggle and to forge a poetic vision out of the very stuff of contradiction, we understand the true heroism of his age. In the course of his long career, Cocteau has brought his own special vision to many aspects of life and art, enriching them and ennobling them in the effort to make life worthy to be lived. He has played a major part in the creation of a theatrical tradition equaled nowhere else in the world. He has tried to express the ethics and emotions of heroism in a world without values. His partial failure is worth many victories. It is the victory of failure, the only kind worth having. It has been earned. Cocteau saw so deeply into history that no one believed him. Perhaps he has even ceased to believe himself. But another prophet of pure poetry understood the depth and significance of Cocteau's hermetic communications. Rainer Maria Rilke commented on Cocteau's casual familiarity with the secret of history in these words: "Tell Cocteau that I love him, for he is the only one who returns bronzed from the world of myth as from the shores of the sea."

Chronology

OF MAJOR PLAYS AND FILMS

Dates are those of first production or release.

PARADE, *ballet réaliste.* Music by Eric Satie, sets and costumes by Pablo Picasso. With the Ballet Russe of Serge Diaghilev. Choreography by Léonide Massine. Rome 1916—Paris 1917.

LE BŒUF SUR LE TOIT ou *The Do Nothing Bar,* pantomime. Music by Darius Milhaud, set by Raoul Dufy. Directed by Cocteau. With the Fratellini clowns. 1920.

LES MARIÉS DE LA TOUR EIFFEL, farce. Costumes and masks by Jean Victor-Hugo. Performed by the Swedish Ballet of Rolf de Maré to music by "Les Six." 1921.

ANTIGONE, adaptation of Sophocles. Music by Arthur Honegger, set by Picasso, costumes by Gabrielle Chanel. With Antonin Artaud, Cocteau and Charles Dullin, who produced the play at the Atelier in 1922.

ROMÉO ET JULIETTE, *prétexte à mise en scène,* in five acts and twenty-three tableaux. Sets and costumes by Hugo. With Marcel Herrand and Andrée Pascal. 1924.

ORPHÉE, tragedy in one act and one interval. Set by Hugo, costumes by Chanel. With Georges and Ludmilla Pitoëff. 1926.

LA VOIX HUMAINE, monologue in one act. Set by Christian Bérard. Created by Berthe Bovy at the Comédie-Française in 1930.

LE SANG D'UN POÈTE, film. Music by Georges Auric. Direction and narration by Cocteau. With Lee Miller, Jean Desbordes and Barbette. 1932.

LA MACHINE INFERNALE, tragedy in four acts. Sets and costumes by Bérard. Produced and directed by Louis Jouvet. With Jean-Pierre Aumont. 1934.

ŒDIPE-ROI, adaptation of Sophocles. Set by Guillaume Monin, costumes by Cocteau. First appearance of Jean Marais in a play of Cocteau's. 1937.

LES CHEVALIERS DE LA TABLE RONDE, play in four acts. Sets by Cocteau, costumes by Chanel. With Jean Marais. 1937.

LES PARENTS TERRIBLES, play in three acts. Sets by Monin. Directed by Alice Cocéa. With Germaine Dermoz, Alice Cocéa, Jean Marais. 1938.

LES MONSTRES SACRÉS, *portrait d'une pièce en trois actes.* Sets by Bérard. Directed by André Brulé. With Yvonne de Bray and Jean Marais. 1940.

LA MACHINE À ÉCRIRE, play in three acts. Set by Jean Marais, who also played two roles. 1941.

RENAUD ET ARMIDE, tragedy in three acts. Sets and costumes by Bérard. Directed by Cocteau. Created at the Comédie-Française in 1943.

LE BARON FANTÔME, film. Produced and directed by Serge de Poligny. Dialogue by Cocteau. 1943.

L'ÉTERNEL RETOUR, film. Music by Auric. Directed by Jean Delannoy. Scenario and dialogue by Cocteau. With Madeleine Solange and Jean Marais. 1944.

LA BELLE ET LA BÊTE, film. Music by Auric, costumes by Bérard. Written and directed by Cocteau. With Josette Day and Jean Marais. 1945.

L'AIGLE À DEUX TÊTES, play in three acts. Music by Auric, sets by André Beaurepaire, costumes by Bérard. With Edwige Feuillère and Jean Marais. 1946.

RUY BLAS, film. Scenario and dialogue by Cocteau. With Danielle Darrieux and Jean Marais. 1947.

LES PARENTS TERRIBLES, film. Music by Auric, set by Bérard. Written, produced and directed by Cocteau. With Josette Day, Yvonne de Bray, Jean Marais. 1948.

L'AIGLE À DEUX TÊTES, film. Music by Auric, sets by Bérard. With Edwige Feuillère and Jean Marais. 1948.

ORPHÉE, film. Music by Auric. Written and directed by Cocteau. With Maria Casarès, Jean Marais, François Périer. 1950.

LES ENFANTS TERRIBLES, film. Directed by Jean-Pierre Melville. Scenario and dialogue by Cocteau. 1950.

BACCHUS, play in three acts. Produced and directed by Jean-Louis Barrault. 1951.

Notes

All quotations or translations are cited from the
eleven-volume edition of *Les Oeuvres complètes
de Jean Cocteau,* Marguerat, Lausanne, 1946–1951,
unless otherwise indicated.

SITUATION OF COCTEAU

1. "Jean Cocteau seems to me to have become a lost soul. . . .
What is disturbing is the awful vacuity of all these pieces, a
deliberate but in no way justified meaninglessness." *In Search
of Theater,* p. 49. Mr. Bentley has treated Cocteau more kindly
in his *The Playwright As Thinker,* pp. 228–232. Yet he con-
cludes by saying that there is a vacuum at the center of Cocteau's
works.

2. *Nouvelles Etudes*, p. 197. Perhaps due to the hostile influence of Gide, who had too much in common with Cocteau to appreciate his merits, the writers of the *Nouvelle Revue Française* would not take Cocteau seriously. Gide's estimate of Cocteau is perhaps indicated by the sinister Robert de Passavant, in *Les Faux-Monnayeurs;* reputed to be a portrait of Cocteau.

3. *Le Mystère laïc*, Vol. 10, p. 34.

4. Vol. 9, p. 293.

5. P. 29.

THE ENTRE DEUX GUERRES

1. *Visites à Maurice Barrès* in *Le Rappel à l'ordre*, Vol. 9, p. 136.

2. *Ibid.*, p. 133.

3. *Ibid.*, p. 143.

4. *Opium*, Vol. 10, p. 65.

5. Quoted by Maurice Nadeau, *Documents Surréalistes* (Editions du Seuil, Paris, 1948), p. 63.

6. *Le Rappel à l'ordre*, Vol. 9, p. 73.

7. Lotte Eisner, *L'Ecran démoniaque* (André Bonne, Paris, 1952), pp. 14–15.

8. I refrain from mentioning Jean Anouilh, who seems to me to be split between the two traditions. In Anouilh's important plays, there is a central character who is preoccupied by the search for some realistic truth. Around him a collection of *grotesques* weave a fantastic web.

9. Mme Magny acknowledges that Jean-Paul Sartre first suggested this analysis of Giraudoux.

10. Vol. 10, p. 28.

11. Quotations in this paragraph are from *Le Rappel à l'ordre*, Vol. 9, p. 191; *La Difficulté d'être*, p. 89; *Lettre à Jacques Maritain*, Vol. 9, p. 269.

12. *Variété V* (Gallimard, Paris, 1945), p. 159.
13. Note the famous "spell" from the play *Renaud et Armide:*

Thread, thread, thread, unroll your bobbin on my heart.
Pass out from me, thread, thread, thread. Thread which runs,
    thread which floats,
Look at the profile of that proud man.
Weave your web about Renaud, thread, thread, thread.
Let us forget, thread, thread, thread, my disdained soul
I must be nothing here but your humble spider.
Thread, thread, thread, let us hurry to catch him in the net.
How beautiful you are! How ugly he is!
How I love your suppleness and your serpent's cold,
With what care my heart watches over your masterpiece.
Fierce thread, hard thread, pure thread, luminous thread,
My love collaborates in the least of your knots.
It guesses your path. It crosses, it knots, it weaves.
Till around Renaud my circle grows smaller,
Till I pass, repass, and until I touch
That man whom we must attach in the center.

(Act II, scene 3)

14. *Portraits-Souvenirs,* Vol. 11, p. 16.
15. Vol. 9, p. 288.

THEATER AS PARADE

1. *Portraits-Souvenirs,* Vol. 11, p. 40.
2. *Ibid.,* p. 59.
3. *Ibid.,* p. 36.
4. Quotations in this paragraph are from *Portraits-Souvenirs,*
    Vol. 11, p. 60, and *Le Foyer des artistes,* Vol. 11, p. 373.
5. Preface to *Les Mariés de la Tour Eiffel,* Vol. 7, p. 17.

6. The term recurs in two recent works on Cocteau: *L'Etoile de Jean Cocteau* by Jean-Pierre Millecam and *La Dramaturgie de Jean Cocteau* by Pierre Dubourg. Ronald Peacock, *The Poet in the Theater,* adopts the term as does Francis Fergusson in his *The Idea of a Theater.* These critics understand the term in its later sense, that is, as symbolic action or language; they overlook its original reference to the visual surprise or spectacle.

7. Another view on Cocteau's relationship with these painters and musicians whom he claims as his friends is expressed by Maurice Sachs in his *Le Sabbat,* p. 121. Sachs asserts that Cocteau was merely a publicity agent for these people, who tolerated Cocteau, while despising him, because of his ability to present their works to the public. And André Gide has this to say in his *Journal,* p. 688: ". . . went to see *Parade*—one doesn't know whether to admire most its pretention or its poverty. Cocteau is walking in the wings where I go to see him; aging, contracted, miserable. He knows very well that the sets, the costumes, are by Picasso, that the music is by Satie, but he wonders if Picasso and Satie are not by Cocteau."

8. *La Difficulté d'être,* p. 21.

9. *Les Mariés de la Tour Eiffel,* Vol. 7, p. 26.

10. *Ibid.,* p. 13.

11. *Ibid.,* p. 12.

12. *Journal d'un inconnu,* p. 35.

13. *Le Rappel à l'ordre,* Vol. 9, p. 149.

14. Vol. 6, p. 14.

15. These quotations are from *Portraits-Souvenirs,* Vol. 11, p. 41, and *Le Rappel à l'ordre,* Vol. 9, p. 105.

16. *Ibid.,* p. 28.

DREAM AND DISCONTINUITY

1. Quotations are from the scenario, *Le Sang d'un poète,* 1948.
2. C. G. Wallis, "The Blood of a Poet," *Kenyon Review* (Winter 1944), p. 41.
3. Preface to *Le Sang d'un poète,* pp. 13–14.
4. C. G. Wallis, "The Blood of a Poet," p. 38.
5. This and the preceding quotation are from Mrs. Langer's *Feeling and Form* (Scribner's, New York, 1953), pp. 412 and 415.
6. Quotations are from the scenario, *Orphée,* 1951.

ORPHEUS AND ANALOGY

1. *Opium,* Vol. 10, p. 70.

COCTEAU THE HUNTED

1. Vol. 9, pp. 368–369.
2. Claude Mauriac, *Jean Cocteau ou la vérité du mensonge.* Claude Mauriac, like Maurice Sachs, has recanted. He has let it be known that he no longer judges Cocteau so severely. Both these authors seem to have been reacting against their own youthful enthusiasm for Cocteau and his influence on them rather than against the man's works.
3. Pp. 20, 32, 116, 201.
4. *La Jeunesse et le scandale,* Vol. 9, p. 319.
5. Vol. 9, pp. 33, 34, 35.
6. *Journal d'un inconnu,* p. 17.
7. *La Jeunesse et le scandale,* Vol. 9, p. 317.
8. Vol. 10, p. 120.
9. P. 87.

LIBERTY AND THE INFERNAL MACHINE

1. I have noted a few production details, not indicated in the text, from the revival of *La Machine infernale* by Jean Marais in 1954.
2. Christian Bérard, quoted by Cocteau in *Maalesh,* p. 16.
3. Francis Fergusson, *The Idea of a Theater,* p. 200.
4. *Ibid.,* p. 198.
5. *Ibid.,* p. 17. This, of course, is only one level of meaning in *Œdipus Rex,* as Mr. Fergusson points out in his brilliant analysis of that play. See especially pp. 36 ff.
6. Pp. 27, 71, 183, 30.
7. *Journal d'un inconnu,* p. 23.
8. *La Difficulté d'être,* pp. 102–103.
9. *Entretiens autour du cinématographe,* p. 67.
10. This and the preceding quotation are from *Démarche d'un poète,* p. 37.
11. *Journal d'un inconnu,* p. 190.
12. *Ibid.,* p. 73.
13. Jean-Paul Sartre, *L'Etre et le néant* (Gallimard, Paris, 1943), p. 66.
14. *Ibid.,* p. 567.
15. *Ibid.,* p. 566.
16. "Le Pacquet rouge," *Opéra,* Vol. 4, p. 152.

COCTEAU AS MORALIST

1. Preface, *Les Chevaliers de la Table Ronde,* Vol. 6, p. 119.
2. Roger Lannes, *Jean Cocteau,* p. 68.
3. *La Difficulté d'être,* p. 212.
4. *Ibid.,* p. 3.

NEUROSIS AND NATURALISM

1. *Le Rappel à l'ordre,* Vol. 9, p. 246.
2. Preface, *Les Mariés de la Tour Eiffel,* Vol. 7, p. 14.
3. Charles Baudelaire, "Fusées," II, *Journaux intimes.*
4. Raymond Radiguet was only fourteen years old at the time of his meeting with Cocteau. It is hard to reconstruct his personality from what Cocteau and others have said about him, but it seems that he stood for some kind of personal and artistic integrity. Hence he fulfilled for Cocteau the same role as Picasso or Diaghilev. He encouraged Cocteau to resist the temptation of facility and to accept the challenge of the traditional genres. His death deprived Cocteau of his most intimate friend, but it allowed him, as compensation, to invent the legend of Radiguet which has now become part of Cocteau's own mythology.
5. Part of the entry for "vaudeville" in the *Petit Larousse* reads: "Brief play interspersed with couplets. . . . When the comedy with couplets, made famous with Désauglers, Scribe, Labiche, disappeared, the name 'vaudeville' was still applied to any light comedy, cleverly plotted, of broad humor." Although this does not seem very applicable to *Les Parents terribles,* one of the characters actually says: ". . . no vaudeville, none of the plays of Labiche is better plotted than this drama." And Pierre Brisson in his *Le Théâtre des années folles,* p. 120, says of this play: "Using for the first time a technique which during all his youth as the rebellious poet he had repudiated, the author suddenly felt himself at home. He discovered the Bataille-Bernstein melodrama-with-vehemence and comedy à la Robert de Flers. He caught every trick, reknotted the threads with a dexterity that enchanted him."

6. "I often thought of the words which Marguerite Jamois spoke to me in my dressing room after *Les Parents terribles:* 'You will never play any other role.' I refused to believe it. During nights of wartime guard duty I decided to study a role opposed to my natural gifts. The Néron of *Britannicus*." Jean Marais, quoted in Jean Cocteau, *Jean Marais*, p. 40.

7. Pierre Brisson, *Le Théâtre des années folles*, p. 87.

8. Preface, *Les Parents terribles*, Vol. 7, p. 84.

9. This quotation and the preceding are from Cocteau's *Lettre aux Américains*, pp. 70 and 72.

10. *Journal d'un inconnu*, p. 39.

11. *Le Rappel à l'ordre*, Vol. 9, p. 177.

12. P. 48.

THE PARADOX OF THE ACTOR

I am indebted at more than one point in this chapter to Robert J. Nelson, whose excellent Ph.D. thesis, "The Play Within a Play in French Dramatic Literature," Columbia University, 1955, brought many of my own ideas into focus.

1. Eric Bentley, *In Search of Theater*, p. 366.

2. *Maalesh*, pp. 26–27. Cocteau claims that the bitter references to him in Gide's *Journal* are the results of jealousy over the young man in question (probably Marc Allégret). This jealousy, Cocteau claims, was completely unfounded.

POETRY AS CHARM

1. Jean Hytier, *Les Arts de littérature* (Charlot, Paris, 1945), p. 15.

2. *Ibid.*, p. 16.

3. Paul Valéry, *Variété III* (Gallimard, Paris, 1936), p. 16.
4. P. 162.
5. *Journal d'un inconnu*, p. 15.
6. *Le Rappel à l'ordre*, Vol. 9, p. 12.

Selected
Bibliography

Bibliographies of Cocteau's works are to be found in the
book by Margaret Crosland and in the volume by Lannes and
Parisot in the "Poètes d'aujourd'hui" series. Articles
on Cocteau, from 1940 through 1955, are listed in the
Modern Language Association French 7 bibliography, Stechert
Hafner, Inc., New York.

SOME BOOKS BY JEAN COCTEAU:

L'Aigle à deux têtes, Gallimard, Paris, 1948.
Anthologie poétique, Club Français du Livre, Paris, 1951.
Bacchus, Gallimard, Paris, 1952.
La Belle et la bête, journal d'un film, J. B. Janin, Paris, 1946.
Le Chiffre sept, poems, Pierre Seghers, Paris, 1952.
Clair-obscur, poems, Editions du Rocher, Monaco, 1954.
Démarche d'un poète, F. Bruckmann, Munich, 1954.

La Difficulté d'être, Editions du Rocher, Monaco, 1953.

Entretiens autour du cinématographe, Editions André Bonne, Paris, 1951.

Jean Marais, Calmann-Lévy, Paris, 1951.

Journal d'un inconnu, Bernard Grasset, Paris, 1953.

Lettre aux Américains, Bernard Grasset, Paris, 1949.

Maalesh, Gallimard, Paris, 1949.

Œuvres complètes, 11 Vols., Marguerat, Lausanne, 1946–1951.

Orphée, scenario, Editions André Bonne, Paris, 1951.

Le Sang d'un poète, scenario, Editions du Rocher, Monaco, 1948.

Théâtre de poche, Editions Paul Morihien, Paris, 1949.

BOOKS ON COCTEAU:

Crosland, Margaret, *Jean Cocteau,* Peter Nevill, London, 1955.

Dubourg, Pierre, *La Dramaturgie de Jean Cocteau,* Bernard Grasset, Paris, 1954.

Fowlie, Wallace, *Journals of Jean Cocteau,* Criterion Books, New York, 1956. Translated, edited and with introduction.

Lannes, Roger, and Parisot, Henri, *Jean Cocteau,* "Poètes d'aujourd'hui," n. 4, Editions Pierre Seghers, Paris, 1945.

Mauriac, Claude, *Jean Cocteau ou la vérité du mensonge,* Odette Lieutier, Paris, 1945.

Millecam, Jean-Pierre, *L'Etoile de Jean Cocteau,* Editions du Rocher, Monaco, 1952.

REVIEWS OF WHICH AN ENTIRE ISSUE IS
DEVOTED TO COCTEAU:

Empreintes, May-June-July 1950, L'Ecran du Monde, Brussels.
Paris-Théâtre, n. 81, February 1954. Cocteau and Jean Marais.
Romanfilm, Paris, 1946. *L'Eternel Retour.* Story of the film with
  photographs.

BOOKS WHICH REFER TO COCTEAU.
SOME ARTICLES ON COCTEAU:

Bentley, Eric, *In Search of Theater,* Vintage Books, Inc., New York,
  1953.
———, *The Playwright As Thinker,* Reynal and Hitchcock, New
  York, 1946.
Bishop, John Peale, "A Film of Jean Cocteau," *The Collected Essays
  of John Peale Bishop,* Charles Scribner's Sons, New York, 1948.
Boorsch, Jean, "The Use of Myths in Cocteau's Theater," *Yale
  French Studies,* n. 5, 1950.
Brisson, Pierre, *Le Théâtre des années folles,* Editions du Milieu du
  Monde, Geneva, 1943.
Carco, Francis, *De Montmartre au Quartier Latin,* Albin Michel,
  Paris, 1927.
Fergusson, Francis, *The Idea of a Theater,* Princeton University
  Press, Princeton, New Jersey, 1949.
Hoog, Armand, "Pour Cocteau," *La Nef,* n. 52, March 1949, pp.
  93–96.

Mauriac, François, "Lettre ouverte à Jean Cocteau," *Le Figaro littéraire,* December 29, 1951.

Merle, Robert, "Oscar Wilde en prison," *Les Temps modernes,* n. 107, November 1954, pp. 613–636.

Peacock, Ronald, *The Poet in the Theater,* Routledge and Kegan Paul, Ltd., London, 1946.

Pucciani, Oreste F., *The French Theater since 1930,* Ginn and Co., Boston, 1954. Anthology of modern plays, with essay on *La Machine infernale.*

Raymond, Marcel, *De Baudelaire au Surréalisme,* José Corti, Paris, 1947.

Rivière, Jacques, *Nouvelles Etudes,* Gallimard, Paris, 1947.

Sachs, Maurice, *Le Bœuf sur le toit,* Nouvelle Revue Critique, Paris, 1939.

———, *Le Sabbat,* Editions Corrêa, Paris, 1946.

Wallis, C. G., "The Blood of a Poet," *Kenyon Review,* Vol. 6, n. 1, Winter 1944, pp. 24–42.